# General Introduction
## of Britain and America

# 英美国家概况

主　编　何　礼（重庆人文科技学院）
　　　　刘　璐（重庆人文科技学院）
副主编　叶　春（重庆人文科技学院）
　　　　杨静雯（SOAS, University of London）
编　者　（以姓氏笔画为序）
　　　　王博华（四川外国语大学）
　　　　王婷婷（四川仪表工业学校）
　　　　刘　尧（重庆人文科技学院）
　　　　邹　立（重庆人文科技学院）
　　　　蒋晓洁（重庆航天职业技术学院）

重庆大学出版社

U0586726

## 内容提要

本书分为两大部分：第一部分为英国国家概况，第二部分为美国国家概况。英国国家概况部分一共 10 个单元。其中第 1 至第 3 单元为英国主要地理特征，气候特点，以及人口结构等基本信息介绍。第 4 至第 6 单元主要讲述了英国政治经济方面的一些主要特点，分析了其法律设置的基本思想。此部分最后章节主要焦点在英国的文化和教育方面，对其现行教育体制进行了深入的分析研究。美国国家概况部分一共 10 个单元。其中前三个单元主要内容为美国社会基本信息概括，涵盖了美国现行法律及宗教方面的内容。接下来的第 4 至第 6 单元对美国一些基本风俗特点进行了介绍，如饮食文化、家庭文化等。本书最后四个单元主要焦点在美国的文化教育方面，涵盖了媒体、文学等方面的内容。

**图书在版编目(CIP)数据**

英美国家概况/何礼,刘璐主编.--重庆:重庆大学出版社,2017.12(2023.7重印)

ISBN 978-7-5689-0961-7

Ⅰ.①英… Ⅱ.①何…②刘… Ⅲ.①英语—阅读教学—教材②英国—概况③美国—概况 Ⅳ.①H319.4:K

中国版本图书馆 CIP 数据核字(2017)第 316451 号

General Introduction of Britain and America

**英美国家概况**

何礼 刘璐 主 编

责任编辑:杨 琪　　版式设计:杨 琪
责任校对:秦巴达　　责任印制:赵 晟

\*

重庆大学出版社出版发行
出版人:饶帮华
社址:重庆市沙坪坝区大学城西路 21 号
邮编:401331
电话:(023) 88617190　88617185(中小学)
传真:(023) 88617186　88617166
网址:http://www.cqup.com.cn
邮箱:fxk@ cqup.com.cn (营销中心)
全国新华书店经销
POD:重庆新生代彩印技术有限公司

\*

开本:787mm×1092mm　1/16　印张:10　字数:184千
2017 年 12 月第 1 版　2023 年 7 月第 7 次印刷
ISBN 978-7-5689-0961-7　定价:35.00 元

本书如有印刷、装订等质量问题,本社负责调换
版权所有,请勿擅自翻印和用本书
制作各类出版物及配套用书,违者必究

# 前　言

　　"英美国家概况"课程是英语专业学生必修的一门基础知识课程,目的是让学生熟悉英国和美国的历史、经济、文化、教育、社会习俗、自然地理等一般知识,丰富文化修养,加深对英语语言和文学的理解,提高分析与辨别的能力。

　　按照教育部21世纪我国高等学校英语专业人才的培养目标和规格要求,编者希望通过本书引导学生在打好扎实的英语语言基本功和牢固掌握英语专业知识的前提下,拓宽人文学科知识面,并对英国和美国社会文化、政治、经济、历史和科技教育等有较全面的了解。

　　本书分为两大部分:第Ⅰ部分为英国国家概况,第Ⅱ部分为美国国家概况。

　　英国国家概况部分一共10个单元。其中第1至第3单元为英国主要地理特征,气候特点,以及人口结构等基本信息介绍。同时,该部分还对英国历史及其宗教特点进行了相应的总结。第4至第6单元主要讲述了英国政治经济方面的一些主要特点,分析了其法律设置的基本思想。此部分最后章节主要焦点在英国的文化和教育方面,对其现行教育体制进行了深入的分析研究。

　　美国国家概况部分一共10个单元。其中前3个单元的主要内容为美国社会基本信息概括,涵盖了美国现行法律及宗教方面的内容。在接下来的4、5、6单元中,作者对美国一些基本风俗特点进行了介绍,如饮食文化、家庭文化等。本书最后4个单元主要焦点在美国的文化教育方面,涵盖了媒体、文学等方面的内容。

　　何礼和刘尧负责全书的编写框架设计工作,并对全书进行了认真、细致的修改和校对。邹立、王婷婷、王博华对全书进行了润色,并对编写小故事、讨论题等方面提出了许多宝贵的修改意见。

　　本书各章节具体分工如下:

　　何　礼:美国部分第11、12、13、14、15、16单元全部。

　　刘　尧:美国部分第17、18、19、20单元全部,英国部分第3、7单元问题。

　　刘　璐:英国部分第1、2单元全部,第4单元正文。

　　叶　春:英国部分第5、6单元全部,第10单元正文。

杨静雯：英国部分第 3、7 单元正文，第 8、9 单元全部。

蒋晓洁：英国部分第 4、10 单元问题。

由于编者的水平和经验的限制，错误和缺点在所难免，欢迎读者批评指正。

编　者

2017 年 8 月

# Table of Contents

# Table of Contents

# Part I

# The Great Britain

## Unit 1

# Geographical Features

The full name of the country we are studying is the United Kingdom of Great Britain and Northern Ireland. Strictly speaking, the British Isles, Great Britain and England are all geographical names. They are not the official name of the country. The British Isles are made up of two large islands and hundreds of small ones. The two large islands are Great Britain and Ireland. Great Britain is the larger of these two islands. It forms the United Kingdom with Northern Ireland—the northern part of Ireland. So the official name of the United Kingdom is the United Kingdom of Great Britain and Northern Ireland. But it is too much of a mouthful to say such a long name for a country, so people just say Britain, the United Kingdom or simple UK. This is one country on the British Isles and its capital is London.

Britain is an island country. It is surrounded by the sea. It lies in the North Atlantic Ocean off the north coast of Europe. It is separated from the rest of Europe by the English Channel in the south and the North Sea in the east. The English Channel between England and France is quite narrow and the narrowest part is called the Straits of Dover, which is only 33 km across. In 1985 the British government and the French government decided to build a channel tunnel under the Straits of Dover so that England and France could be joined together by road. After 8 years of hard work, this channel tunnel which is called "Chunnel" was open to traffic in May 1994.

Britain covers an area of 244,820 square km. It runs 1,000 km from north to south and extends at the widest part about 500 km. So no part of Britain is very far from the coast and it provides a valuable resource. The British coast is long and has good, deep harbors. Sea routes extend far inland, providing cheap transportation.

Britain has, for centuries, been slowly tilting with the North-West slowly rising and the South-East slowly sinking. The north and west of Britain are mainly highlands. In western parts of Scotland this rise in the land has resulted in the formation of raised beaches—flat areas of land in an otherwise mountainous area, which provide the main farming, settlements, and industrial areas as well as route ways. The east and south-east are mostly lowland. They are part of the Great European Plain, with its level land and fertile soil. There is much good farmland especially in the south and along the east coast of England.

England occupies the largest, southern part of Great Britain with Wales to its west and Scotland to its north. It covers an area of 130,423 square km which takes up nearly 60% of the whole island. The south-west and west except for the Severn Valley and the Cheshire-Lancashire Plain (round Liverpool) are largely a plateau, with rolling plains, downs and occasional moors. The Pennies, a range of hill running from North Midlands to the Scottish border, are the principal mountain chain. But the highest peak of England, Scafell (978 m), is in the Lake District in North-West England. The east of England is mainly an open cultivated plain, narrowing in North Yorkshire to a passage between coastal moors and the Pennies, and in Northumberland to a coastal strip.

Scotland has an area of 77,080 square kilometers. It is in the north of Great Britain with many mountains, lakes and islands. There are three natural zones: the Highlands in the north, the central Lowlands, and the southern Uplands. The Highlands are a wild, rocky, mountainous plateau with a coast-line deeply indented, especially in the west. Ben Nevis (1,343 m), the highest mountain in Britain is located here. The western part of Highlands and islands of Hebrides are a very beautiful region. Great sea-lochs, or fiords, alternate with wild and empty hills, and on some of the lochs there are farms which can only be reached by boat. The Lowlands in the centre comprise mostly the Forth and Clyde Valleys, coal and iron fields and dairy pasture. This is the most important area in Scotland which contains most of the industry and population. The southern Uplands, a rolling moorland, are cut by small fertile river valleys. Scotland has about 800 islands including the Orkneys, Shetlands, Hebrides and hundreds of lakes. Edinburgh is the capital city of Scotland.

Wales is in the west of Great Britain. It has an area of 20,776 square km which takes up less than 9% of the whole island. Most of Wales is mountainous: the hills rise steeply from the sea and are rather flat on top. 6% of Wales is covered with forest and much of the country is pasture-land for sheep and cattle. Only 12% of the land is arable. Wales forms a massif with a lowland fringe widest along the English border and south coast. The massif is largely between 180~600 m, rocky in the north and coal bearing in the south. Snowdonia (1,085 m) in the northwest is the highest mountain in Wales. The capital of Wales is Cardiff.

Northern Ireland is a fourth region of the United Kingdom. It takes up the northern fifth of Ireland and has an area of 14,147 square km. It has a rocky and wild northern coastline, with several deep indentations. In the north-east lie the uplands of Country Antrim, while the mountains in the south-east gradually give way to the central lowlands of the Lough Neagh basin. Belfast is the capital of Northern Ireland.

Rivers in Britain do not freeze in winter. They play a very important role in the country's economy. The great ports of London, Liverpool and Glasgow are all connected to the sea by rivers. Besides, the Tweed, the Tyne, the Tees, and the Thames rivers on the east coast all face North Sea ports on the European continent. They are also close to rich fishing grounds. On the west coast the Clyde, the Mersey, and the Severn rivers carry raw materials to busy manufacturing cities inland. The rivers in Britain are not very large. The longest river is the Severn River which is only 338 km long. It rises in central Wales and flows in a semicircle through West Central England to the Bristol Channel. The second longest and most important river in Britain is the Thames River. It is 336 km long. It rises in the Cotswolds in southwest England and flows through the Midlands of England to London and out into the North Sea. The Thames flows rather slowly, which is very favorable for water transportation. Ocean-going ships can sail up it as far as London and small ships can sail up it for further 138 km. Oxford is also on the Thames. River Clyde is the most important river in Scotland. It rises in Dumfries and runs 171 km, passing through Glasgow, and enters the Firth of Clyde. It is an important commercial waterway.

There are many lakes in Britain especially in northern Scotland, the Lake District in north-west England and North Wales. However, the largest lake in Britain is the Lough Neagh in Northern Ireland which covers an area of 396 square kilometers. The Lake District is one of the most popular tourist attractions in Britain. It is well known for its wild and beautiful scenery and 15 lakes. The largest ones are Windermere, Ullswater, Derwentwater and Coniston Water. It was also the home of the Lake Poets—William Wordsworth, Samuel Taylor Coleridge and Robert Southey of the 19th century Britain.

When we say climate we mean the average weather conditions in a certain place over a period of years. We do not mean the day-to-day weather conditions in a certain place. Though it seems that people are always complaining about the weather in Britain because it is rainy and so changeable and unpredictable, the climate in Britain is in fact a favorable one. It has a favorable maritime climate—winters are mild, not too cold and summers are cool, not too hot, and it has a steady reliable rainfall throughout the whole year. It has a small range of temperature. The average temperature in winter in the north is 4~6 ℃. and in summer in the south is 12~17 ℃. So even in winter one can still see stretches of green grass in the open country, in the parks and around the houses.

Britain has a mild temperature and plenty of rainfall, but areas sharing the same latitude with it have different climates. What are the factors that have a determining influence on the character of the English weather and climate?

The shores of the British Isles, especially the western shores, are bathed by a warm drift of water, the North Atlantic Drift which is a continuation of the Gulf Stream. The existence of this large warm drift of sea water undoubtedly has an important effect in moderating winter conditions in

Britain. To the north and north-east of the British Isles, no land barrier exists to prevent the flow of the warm drift. The British Isles thus lie within the warm embrace of this well-known warm stream.

Except, perhaps, for certain periods in winter, the British Isles lie wholly within what has long been called the westerly wind belt. The south-westerly wind is the dominant wind in Britain. Since it comes from the Atlantic Ocean, it is always mild and moist.

The configuration of Britain, particularly the existence of numerous inlets, makes the penetration inland of oceanic influences more effective than would otherwise be the case.

Of course there are some other contributing factors, but the above-mentioned factors are considered the most important ones.

## ▶ A Short Story ◀

### English Channel

English Channel, also called The Channel, French La Manche, looks like a narrow arm of the Atlantic Ocean separating the southern coast of England from the northern coast of France and tapering eastward to its junction with the North Sea at the Strait of Dover (French: Pas de Calais). With an area of some 29,000 square miles (75,000 square km), it is the smallest of the shallow seas covering the continental shelf of Europe. From its mouth in the North Atlantic Ocean—an arbitrary limit marked by a line between the Scilly Isles and the Isle of Ushant—its width gradually narrows from 112 miles (180 km) to a minimum of 21 miles(33 km), while its average depth decreases from 400 to 150 feet (120 to 45 m). Although the English Channel is a feature of notable scientific interest, especially in regard to tidal movements, its location has given it immense significance over the centuries, as both a route and a barrier during the peopling of Britain and the emergence of the nation-states of modern Europe. The current English name (in general use since the early 18th century) probably derives from the designation "canal" in Dutch sea atlases of the late 16th century. Earlier names included Oceanus Britannicus and the British Sea, and the French have regularly used La Manche (in reference to the sleevelike coastal outline) since the early 17th century.

## *••• Exercises •••*

【Fill in the Blanks】

1. The full name of the United Kingdom is _____.

2. The island of Great Britain is made up of England, _____ and _____.

3. The narrowest part of English Channel is called _____.

4. England occupies the largest, _____ part of the Great Britain.

【Multiple Choices】

1. There are _____ political divisions on the island of Great Britain.

   A. one        B. two        C. four        D. three

2. The British Isles are mainly made up of _____.

   A. England and Ireland

   B. England, Scotland and Wales

   C. Great Britain and Northern Ireland

   D. Great Britain and Ireland

3. Which is the largest city in Scotland?

   A. Cardiff.        B. Edinburgh.        C. Glasgow.        D. Manchester.

4. The north and west of Britain are mainly _____.

   A. level land        B. farmland        C. highlands        D. lowlands

5. Ben Nevis, the highest mountain in Britain, is located in _____.

   A. England                     B. Wales

   C. Scotland                  D. Northern Ireland

【Discussion】

1. Describe the geographical position of Britain.

2. What are the main factors which influence the climate in Britain?

   C. England, Scotland, Wales and Ireland

## Unit 2

# People and Religion

Britain has a population of 61,383 million (2016). This is a very large population for such a small country. So it is a densely populated country with an average of 237 people per square km and it is very unevenly distributed. 90% of the population is urban and only 10% is rural, i. e. most people live in the cities and towns and only a few live in the country. On the other hand, there are some quite large tracts of barren, hilly country, especially in Northern Scotland, which are almost uninhabited.

There is a great concentration of population in England, with 80% of its population living in cities, and only 2% of the population working in agriculture. Its largest city is the capital, London, which is dominant in the UK in all fields: government, finance, and culture. England is physically the largest of the four nations, and it has by far the largest population. This dominance in size is reflected in a cultural and economic dominance. It has the result that people in foreign countries sometimes make the mistake of talking about England when they mean the UK. Significantly, people in England sometimes make that mistake too, but people in the other three nations would not: they might call themselves British (as might the English), or they might call themselves Scottish or Welsh or Irish, but they certainly wouldn't call themselves (or lie to be called) English. So oddly, of the four nations, the English feel most British and therefore have the weakest sense of themselves as a separate "English" culture within Britain.

The population of Britain is made up mainly of the English (81.5%), the Scottish (9.6%), the Welsh (1.9%), the Irish (2.4%), the Northern Irish (1.8%) and other peoples (2.8%).

Today British people move around the country more than they used to. Northerners come to live in the south and Southerners and East Anglians go to the north. Lots of Scots, Welsh and Irish come and live in England. They take on each other's way of life and this makes it more difficult for people to distinguish between people from different parts of Britain. However, differences in regional character and speech can still be seen and heard. In fact in some regions people are doing all they can to preserve their own language and culture.

The English are Anglo-Saxons, but the Scots, Welsh and Irish are Celts. The Celts were different groups of ancient people who came originally from Germany and spread through France, Spain and Britain. The Celts came to Britain after 700 B.C. When they came, one group was called Britons and from this group the people of Britain grew. Later they were conquered by the Romans. During the 5th century when the Roman Empire fell, the Germanic Angles and Saxons invaded and conquered Britain. The Germanic conquerors gave England its name "Angle" land. During the 9th century, Britain was invaded by the Danes or Vikings and in 1066 by the Norman French. It was from the union of Norman conquerors and the defeated Anglo-Saxons that the English people and the English language were born. Today the names of most English people still bear the trace of their ancestors. The commonest English name "Smith" comes from the German name "Schmidt" and some English families have Norman French names such as D'Arcy, Beaufort and Beauchamp. It is estimated that there are about 800,000 people called Smith in England and Wales.

The ancestors of the Welsh were the ancient Britons who escaped from the invading Angles and Saxons and found shelter in the wild mountains of Wales. The Celts of Wales defended their freedom for 1,000 years and were not conquered by the English until 1536. Today about a quarter of the Welsh population still speak Welsh as their first language and about one per cent speak only Welsh. Welsh is an ancient Celtic language. It was given equality with English for all official use in Wales in 1965. So many school children have to learn Welsh and most public sings are in Welsh as well as in English.

Welsh is quite different from English and Welsh names are different too.

The Welsh are emotional and cheerful people. They are music lovers and are proud of their past. Throughout the year they have festivals of song and dance and poetry called Eisteddfodau. The great event of the year is the National Eisteddfod. On these occasions competitions are held in Welsh poetry, music, singing and art and in this way they keep the Welsh language and Welsh culture alive.

Some Germanic Angles settled in the Scottish lowlands and in the borderlands between Scotland and England, but they never invaded the Highlands, where the Scots remained safe in their mountain glens and on their islands. Scots are proud that the English never conquered them. Though the Scots are said to be a serious, cautious and thrifty people, today most visitors to Scotland come away with an impression that they are hospitable, generous and friendly.

Hundreds of years ago, Scots and English Protestants were sent to live in Northern Ireland. Since then there has been bitter fighting between the Protestants who are the dominant group, and the Roman Catholics, who are seeking more social, political and economic opportunities. The British Government and the Government of Ireland (Eire) are now working together to bring peace to Northern Ireland.

Irish, often called Erse, is a form of Gaelic. It is the official first language of the Republic of Ireland and English is the second. The Irish are known for their charm and vivacity as well as for the beauty of their Irish girls.

Religion in the United Kingdom and in the countries that preceded it has been dominated, for over 1,400 years, by various forms of Christianity. Religious affiliations of United Kingdom citizens are recorded by regular surveys, the four major ones being the UK Census, the Labor Force Survey, the British Social Attitudes Survey and the European Social Survey. According to the 2011 UK census, Christianity is the major religion, followed by Islam, Hinduism, Sikhism, Judaism and Buddhism in terms of number of adherents. Among Christians, Anglicans are the most common denomination, followed by Roman Catholics. This, and the relatively large number of individuals with nominal or no religious affiliations, has led commentators to variously describe the United Kingdom as a multi-faith and secularized society.

The United Kingdom was formed by the union of previously independent countries from 1707, and consequently most of the largest religious groups do not have UK-wide organizational structures. While some groups have separate structures for the individual countries of the United Kingdom, others may have a single structure covering England and Wales or Great Britain. Similarly, due to the relatively recent creation of Northern Ireland in 1921, most major religious groups in Northern Ireland are organized on an all-Ireland basis.

While the United Kingdom as a whole lacks an official religion, the Church of England remains the state church of its largest constituent country, England. The Monarch of the United Kingdom is the Supreme Governor of the Church, and accordingly, only a Protestant may inherit the British throne.

Society in the United Kingdom is markedly more secular than it was in the past and the number of churchgoers fell over the second half of the 20th century. In 2012 about 6% of the population of the United Kingdom regularly attended church, with the average age of attendees being 51; in contrast, in 1980, 11% had regularly attended, with an average age of 37. It is predicted that by 2020 attendance will be around 4%, with an average age of 56. This decline in church attendance has forced many churches to close down across the United Kingdom, with the Church of England alone closing 1,500 churches between 1969 and 2002. Their fates include dereliction, demolition, and residential, artistic and commercial conversion. Christians will be a minority in the UK by the middle of this century amid surging growth in atheism and Islam, an authoritative new study charting the future of the world's religions predicts. According to projections by the US-based Pew Research Centre, the proportion of the British population identifying themselves as Christian will reduce by almost a third by 2050 to stand at just 45.4 per cent, compared with almost two thirds in 2010.

One study showed that in 2004 at least 930,000 Muslims attended a mosque at least once a week, just outnumbering the 916,000 regular churchgoers in the Church of England. Most Muslim immigrants to the United Kingdom came from former colonies. The biggest groups of Muslims are of Pakistani, Bangladeshi, Indian and Arab origins, with the remainder coming from Muslim-dominated areas such as Southwest Asia, Somalia, Malaysia, and Indonesia. Muslim sources claim the number of practicing. Muslims is underestimated as nearly all of them pray at home. The number of Muslims in Britain is predicted to more than double to 11.3 per cent, or one in nine of the total population during that time.

The history of the Jews in England goes back to the reign of William the Conqueror. The first written record of Jewish settlement in England dates from 1070. The Jewish presence continued until King Edward I's *Edict of Expulsion* in 1290. British Jews number around 300,000 with the United Kingdom having the fifth largest Jewish community worldwide and being home to the second largest Jewish population in Europe. However, this figure did not include Jews who identified "by ethnicity only" in England and Wales or Scottish Jews who identified as Jewish by upbringing but held no current religion. Jews faced anti-Semitism and stereotypes in Britain, and anti-Semitism "in most cases went along with German phobia" to the extent that Jews were equated with Germans in the early 20th century. This led many Jewish families to anglicize their often German-sounding names. Regardless of some growing anti-Semitism during the 1930s, it was counterbalanced by strong support for British Jews in their local communities.

Though the main political parties are secular, the formation of the Labor Party was influenced by Christian socialism and by leaders from a nonconformist background. In the early 21st century, the *Racial and Religious Hatred Act 2006* made it an offence in England and Wales to incite hatred against a person on the grounds of their religion. The common law offences of blasphemy and blasphemous libel were abolished with the coming into effect of the *Criminal Justice* and *Immigration Act 2008* on July 8th, 2008.

Global study predicts one in nine Britons will be Muslim by 2050 but UK set to become one of the least religious countries in the world overall. It is worth noting that faith in politicians, government, the mainstream media and in many other institutions has diminished, yet the human search for meaning, identity and principles has not gone away as Richard Jenkins states "identity is a process of negotiating relationships of similarity and difference".

## ▶ A Short Story ▶

### Six Things You May Not Know about William the Conqueror

1. He was of Viking extraction.

Though he spoke a dialect of French and grew up in Normandy, a fiefdom loyal to the French kingdom, William and other Normans descended from Scandinavian invaders. William's great-great-great-grandfather, Rollo, pillaged northern France with fellow Viking raiders in the late 9th and early 10th centuries, eventually accepting his own territory (Normandy, named for the Norsemen who controlled it) in exchange for peace.

2. He had reason to hate his original name.

The product of an affair between Robert I, duke of Normandy, and a woman called Herleva, William was likely known to his contemporaries as William the Bastard for much of his life. His critics continued to use this moniker (albeit behind his back) even after he defeated the English at the Battle of Hastings and earned an upgrade to William the Conqueror.

3. His future bride wanted nothing to do with him at first.

When William asked for the hand of Matilda of Flanders, a granddaughter of France's King Robert II, she demurred, perhaps because of his illegitimacy or her entanglement with another man. According to legend, the snubbed duke tackled Matilda in the street, pulling her off her horse by her long braids. In any event, she consented to marry him and bore him 10 children before her death in 1083, which plunged William into a deep depression.

4. He couldn't bear any disrespect toward his mother.

During William's siege of Alençon, a disputed town on the border of Normandy, in the late 1040s or early 1050s, residents are said to have hung animal hides on their walls. They mocked him for being the grandson of a tanner, referring to the occupation of his mother's father. To avenge her honor, he had their hands and feet cut off.

5. He made England speak Franglais.

William spoke no English when he ascended the throne, and he failed to master it despite his efforts. (Like most nobles of his time, he also happened to be illiterate.) Thanks to the Norman invasion, French was spoken in England's courts for centuries and completely transformed the English language, infusing it with new words.

6. His jester was the first casualty of the Battle of Hastings.

William's jester rode beside him during the invasion of England, lifting the troops' spirits by singing about heroic deeds. When they reached enemy lines, he taunted the English by juggling his sword and was promptly killed, initiating the historic skirmish.

## ▪▪▪ Exercises ▪▪▪

【Fill in the Blanks】

1. The Anglo-Saxons began to settle in Britain in the _____ century.

2. Both the Scottish and Welsh people elect their members of parliaments to the London Parliament and each holds _____ and _____ seats respectively.

3. British recorded history begins with the _____ invasion.

4. King Edward was far more _____ than _____ and soon upset his father-in-law.

5. _____, the great Roman General, invaded Britain for the first time in 55 B.C.

【Multiple Choices】

1. The first known settles of Britain were _____.

   A. the Jutes    B. the Celts    C. the Saxons    D. the Iberians

2. In 597, _____ was remarkably successful in converting the king and the

nobility.

　A. Offa　　　　　B. Augustine　　　C. Egbert　　　　　D. Columba

3. For nearly _____ years, Britain was under the Roman occupation.

　A. 100　　　　　B. 200　　　　　C. 300　　　　　D. 400

4. _____ had been created as a northern stronghold.

　A. Bath　　　　　B. York　　　　　C. Carlisle　　　　　D. Newcastle

5. The Norman Conquest of _____ is perhaps the best-known event in English history.

　A. 1063　　　　　B. 1064　　　　　C. 1065　　　　　D. 1066

【Discussion】

1. What is the difference between the ancestors of the English and Scots, Welsh and Irish?

2. Make a brief summary on the religions in the UK.

# Unit 3

# History

The history of the United Kingdom as a unified sovereign state began in 1707 with the political union of the kingdoms of England and Scotland, into a united kingdom called Great Britain. A further *Act of Union* in 1800 added the Kingdom of Ireland to create the United Kingdom of Great Britain and Ireland.

The first decades were marked by Jacobite risings which ended with defeat for the Stuart cause at Culloden in 1746. In 1763, victory in the Seven Years' War led to the dominance of the British Empire, which was to be the foremost global power for over a century and grew to become the largest empire in history. As a result, the culture of the United Kingdom, and its industrial, political, constitutional, educational and linguistic influence, became worldwide.

In 1922, following the *Anglo-Irish Treaty*, most of Ireland seceded to become the Irish Free State; a day later, Northern Ireland seceded from the Free State and returned to the United Kingdom. As a result, in 1927 the United Kingdom changed its formal title to the "United Kingdom of Great Britain and Northern Ireland," usually shortened to "Britain" and (after 1945) to the "United Kingdom" or "UK".

After the Second World War, Britain no longer had the wealth to maintain an empire, so it granted independence to most of the Empire. The new states typically joined the Commonwealth of Nations. The United Kingdom has been a leading member of the United Nations, the European Union and NATO(The North Atlantic Treaty Organization). Since the 1990s large-scale devolution movements in Northern Ireland, Scotland and Wales have changed the political structure of the country.

The Kingdom of Great Britain came into being on May 1st, 1707, as a result of the political union of the Kingdom of England (which included Wales) and the Kingdom of Scotland. The terms of the union had been negotiated the previous year, and laid out in the *Treaty of Union*. The parliaments of Scotland and of England then each ratified the treaty via respective *Acts of Union*. The union was valuable to England's security because Scotland relinquished first, the right to choose a different monarch on Anne's death and second, the right to independently ally with a European power, which could then use Scotland as a base for the invasion of England.

Although now a single kingdom, certain aspects of the former independent kingdoms remained separate, as agreed in the terms in the *Treaty of Union*. Scottish and English law remained separate, as did the Presbyterian Church of Scotland and the Anglican Church of England. England and Scotland also continued to each have its own system of education.

The creation of Great Britain happened during the War of the Spanish Succession, in which just before his death in 1702 William III had reactivated the Grand Alliance against France. His successor, Anne, continued the war. The Duke of Marlborough won a series of brilliant victories over the French, England's first major battlefield successes on the Continent since the Hundred Years War. France was nearly brought to its knees by 1709, when King Louis XIV made a desperate appeal to the French people. Afterwards, his general Marshal Villars managed to turn the tide in favor of France. A more peace-minded government came to power in Great Britain, and the treaties of Utrecht and Rastadt in 1713−1714 ended the war.

At the threshold to the 19th century, Britain was challenged again by France under Napoleon, in a struggle that, unlike previous wars, represented a contest of ideologies between the two nations: the constitutional monarchy of Great Britain versus the liberal principles of the French Revolution ostensibly championed by the Napoleonic Empire. It was not only Britain's position on the world stage that was threatened: Napoleon threatened invasion of Britain itself, and with it, a fate similar to the countries of continental Europe that his armies had overrun.

Events that culminated in the union with Ireland had spanned several centuries. Invasions from England by the ruling Normans from 1170 led to centuries of strife in Ireland and successive Kings of England sought both to conquer and pillage Ireland, imposing their rule by force throughout the entire island. In the early 17th century, large-scale settlement by Protestant settlers from both Scotland and England began, especially in the province of Ulster, seeing the displacement of many of the native Roman Catholic Irish inhabitants of this part of Ireland. Since the time of the first Norman invaders from England, Ireland has been subject to control and regulation, firstly by England then latterly by Great Britain.

The legislative union of Great Britain and Ireland was brought about by the Act of Union 1800, creating the "United Kingdom of Great Britain and Ireland". The Act was passed in both the Parliament of Great Britain and the Parliament of Ireland, dominated by the Protestant Ascendancy and lacking representation of the country's Roman Catholic population. Substantial majorities were achieved, and according to contemporary documents this was assisted by bribery in the form of the awarding of peerages and honors to opponents to gain their votes. Under the terms of the merger, the separate Parliaments of Great Britain and Ireland were abolished, and replaced by a united Parliament of the United Kingdom. Ireland thus became an integral part of the United Kingdom, sending around 100 MPs to the House of Commons at Westminster and 28 representative peers to the House of Lords, elected from among their numbers by the Irish peers themselves, except that Roman Catholic peers were not permitted to take their seats in the Lords. Part of the trade-off for the Irish Catholics was to be the granting of Catholic Emancipation, which had been fiercely resisted by the all-Anglican Irish Parliament. However, this was blocked by King George III, who argued that emancipating the Roman Catholics would breach his Coronation Oath. The Roman Catholic hierarchy had endorsed the Union. However, the decision to block Catholic Emancipation fatally undermined the appeal of the Union.

Britain entered the war because of its implicit support for France, which had entered to support Russia, which in turn had entered to support Serbia. Even more important than that chain of links was Britain's determination to honor its commitment to defend Belgium. Britain was loosely part of the Triple Entente with France and Russia, which (with smaller allies) fought the Central Powers of Germany, Austria and the Ottoman Empire. On other fronts, the British, French, Australians, and Japanese seized Germany's colonies. Britain fought the Ottoman Empire, suffering defeats in the Gallipoli Campaign and in Mesopotamia, while arousing the Arabs who helped expel the Turks from their lands. Exhaustion and war-weariness were growing worse in 1917, as the fighting in France continued with no end in sight. The German spring offensives of 1918 failed, and with the summer arrival of American soldiers at a rate of 10,000 per day, the Germans realized they were being overwhelmed. Germany agreed to a surrender on November 11th, 1918.

The Great Depression originated in the United States in late 1929 and quickly spread to the world. Britain had never experienced the boom that had characterized the U.S., Germany, Canada and Australia in the 1920s, so its bust appeared less severe. Britain's world trade fell in half (1929-1933), the output of heavy industry fell by a third, employment profits plunged in nearly all sectors. At the depth in summer 1932, registered unemployed numbered 3.5 million, and many more had only part-time employment. In 1936, by which time unemployment was lower, 200 unemployed men made a highly publicized march from Jarrow to London in a bid to show the plight of the industrial poor. Unemployment remained high until the war absorbed all the job seekers.

Britain, along with the dominions and the rest of the Empire, declared war on Nazi Germany in 1939, after the German invasion of Poland. After a quiet period of "phoney war", the French and British armies collapsed under German onslaught in spring 1940. The British with the thinnest of margins rescued its main army from Dunkirk (as well as many French soldiers), leaving all their equipment and war supplies behind. Winston Churchill came to power, promising to fight the Germans to the very end. The Germans threatened an invasion—which the Royal Navy was prepared to repel. The war was very expensive. It was paid for by high taxes, by selling off assets, and by accepting large amounts of Lend Lease from the U.S. and Canada. The U.S. gave $40 billion in munitions; Canada also gave aid. (The American and Canadian aid did not have to be repaid, but there were also American loans that were repaid.) Britain was a winner in the war, but it lost India in 1947 and nearly all the rest of the Empire by 1960. It debated its role in world affairs and joined the United Nations in 1945, NATO in 1949, where it became a close ally of the United States. Prosperity returned in the 1950s and London remained a world centre of finance and culture, but the nation was no longer a major world power. In 1973, after a long debate and initial rejection, it joined the European Union.

On September 11th, 1997 (on the 700th anniversary of the Scottish victory over the English at the Battle of Stirling Bridge), a referendum was held on establishing a devolved Scottish Parliament. This resulted in an overwhelming "yes" vote both to establishing the parliament and granting it limited tax varying powers. One week later, a referendum in Wales on establishing a Welsh Assembly was also approved but with a very narrow majority. The first elections were held, and these bodies began to operate in 1999. The creation of these bodies has widened the differences between the countries of the United Kingdom, especially in areas like healthcare. It has also brought to the fore the so-called West Lothian question which is a complaint that devolution for Scotland and Wales but not England has created a situation where all the MPs in the UK parliament can vote on matters affecting England alone but on those same matters Scotland and Wales can make their own decisions.

On 20 February 2016, British Prime Minister David Cameron announced that a referendum on the UK's membership of the European Union would be held on June 23rd, 2016, following years of campaigning by eurosceptics. Debates and campaigns by parties supporting both "Remain" and "Leave" focused on concerns regarding trade and the single market, security, migration and sovereignty. The result of the referendum was in favor of the country leaving the EU with 51.9% of voters wanting to leave. The UK remains a member for the time being, but is expected to invoke *Article 50* of the *Lisbon Treaty*, which would begin negotiations on a withdrawal agreement that will last no more than two years (unless the Council and the UK agree to extend the negotiation period) which will ultimately lead to an exit from the European Union.

## ▰ A Short Story ▰

### Seven Years' War

The Seven Years' War was a global conflict fought between 1756 and 1763. It involved every European great power of the time and spanned five continents, affecting Europe, the Americas, West Africa, India, and the Philippines. The conflict split Europe into two coalitions, led by the Kingdom of Great Britain (including Prussia, Portugal, Hanover, and other small German states) on one side and the Kingdom of France (including the Austrian-led Holy Roman Empire, the Russian Empire, Bourbon Spain, and Sweden) on the other. Meanwhile, in India, the Mughal Empire, with the support of the French, tried to crush a British attempt to conquer Bengal.

Although Anglo-French skirmishes over their American colonies had begun with what became the French and Indian War in 1754, the large-scale conflict that drew in most of the European powers was centered on Austria's desire to recover Silesia from the Prussians. Seeing the opportunity to curtail Britain's and Prussia's ever-growing might, France and Austria put aside their ancient rivalry to form a grand coalition of their own, bringing most of the other European powers to their side. Faced with this sudden turn of events, Britain aligned itself with Prussia, in a series of political maneuvers known as the Diplomatic Revolution. However, French efforts ended in failure when the Anglo-Prussian coalition prevailed, and Britain's rise as among the world's predominant powers destroyed France's supremacy in Europe, thus altering the European balance of power.

## **▪▪▪** *Exercises* **▪▪▪**

【Fill in the Blanks】

1. The first King of the House of Plantagenet was _____.

2. In Henry's day, a jury was composed of _____ men and the jurors' function was to act as _____, not to hear evidences and give verdict.

3. Black Death was spread through _____ in the 14th century, particularly in _____.

4. _____ and _____ were the two important leaders of the 1381 uprising.

5. Mary was called _____ when 300 Protestants were burnt as heretics.

【Multiple Choices】

1. The barons, under Simon de Montfort, forced the king and his son Prince Edward to accept _____.
   A. the Provisions of Oxford
   B. the Great Charter
   C. the Constitution of Clarendon
   D. the Crusade

2. In 1337 _____ declared a war that was to last for hundred years because _____ refused to recognize his claim.
   A. Henry Ⅲ; the French          B. Edward; the Scots
   C. Philip Ⅳ; the French          D. Edward; the French

3. Queen Mary attempted to forcibly reconvert England to _____.
   A. Protestantism                    B. Humanism
   C. Arminianism                      D. Roman Catholicism

4. In 1653, Oliver Cromwell became _____ of the Commonwealth of England.
   A. King          B. Lord Protector          C. Charles Ⅰ          D. Duke

【Discussion】

1. What role did Britain play in the Second World War?

2. Describe the Hundred Years War.

## Unit 4

# Government and Political Parties

The United Kingdom is a constitutional monarchy: the head of State is a king or a queen. In practice, the Sovereign reigns, but does not rule: the United Kingdom is governed, in the name of the Sovereign, by His or Her Majesty's Government—a body of Ministers who are the leading members of whichever political party the electorate has voted into office, and who are responsible to Parliament.

The system of parliamentary government is not based on a written constitution. There is no written constitution in the United Kingdom, that is, unlike the constitutions of most other countries, the British constitution is not set out in any single document. It is made up of statute law, common law and conventions (Conventions are rules and practices which are not legally enforceable but which are regarded as indispensable to the working of government). The Judiciary determines common law and interprets statutes.

The monarchy is the oldest institution of government, going back to at least the 9th century. The continuity of the monarchy, which has had only a few changes in the direct line of succession in the past 1,000 years, has been broken only once when, between 1649 and 1660, a republic was established. Although the monarchy has survived, it seems that it has no real power today.

They present Sovereign, Queen Elizabeth Ⅱ, born on April 21, 1926, was married to the Prince Philip, the Duke of Edinburgh, on November 20th, 1947. She came to the throne on February 6th, 1952, and was crowned on June 2nd, 1953. Her title in the United Kingdom is: "Elizabeth the Second, by the Grace of God of the United Kingdom of Great Britain and Northern

Ireland and of Her Other Realms and Territories, Queen, Head of the Commonwealth, Defender if the Faith".

Although the seat of the monarchy is in Britain, the Queen is also head of state of a number of Commonwealth states such as Australia, Canada, and New Zealand. In each such state the Queen is represented by a Governor-General, appointed by her on the advice of the ministers of the country concerned and completely independent of the British Government. In British dependent territories the Queen is usually represented by governors, who are responsible to the British Government for the administration of the countries concerned.

The title to the Crown is derived partly from statute and partly from common law ruled of descent. Succession is founded on the hereditary principle. Sons of the Sovereign have precedence over daughters in succeeding to the throne. When a daughter succeeds, she becomes Queen Regnant, and has the same powers as king. The consort of a king takes her husband's rank and style, becoming Queen. Under the *Act of Settlement* of 1700, which formed part of the Revolution Settlement following the events of 1688, only Protestant descendants of a granddaughter of James I of England and VI of Scotland (Princess Sophia, the Electress of Hanover) are eligible to succeed. The order of succession can be altered only by common consent of the countries of the Commonwealth.

The Sovereign succeeds to the throne as soon as his or her predecessor dies: there is no interregnum. He or she is at once proclaimed at an Accession Council. The Sovereign's coronation follows the accession after a convenient interval. The ceremony takes place at Westminster Abbey in London.

The eldest son of Queen Elizabeth II—Prince Charles, Prince of Wales—is the heir to the throne. But when Prince Charles and Princess Diana were divorced, many people suggested that he should stand aside from the succession in favor of his eldest son, Prince William.

The Queen is the symbol of the whole nation. Each year the Queen and other members of the royal family visit many parts of the United Kingdom to inaugurate scientific, industrial, artistic and charitable works of national importance. The Queen pays state visits to foreign governments, accompanied by the Duke of Edinburgh. She also undertakes tours of other countries in the Commonwealth (of which the Queen is the head).

Since April, 1993, the Queen has paid income tax on all her personal income and on that part of the Privy Purse income which is used for private purposes. The Queen also pays tax on any realized capital gains on her private investments and on the private proportion of assets in the Privy Purse.

The United Kingdom is a unitary, not a federal, State. All four countries of the kingdom are represented in the parliament at Westminster. The term "parliament" originally meant a meeting for parley or discussion. Parliament consists of the Sovereign, the House of Lords and the House of Commons. The three elements meet together only on occasions of symbolic significance such as the state opening of Parliament, when the Commons are summoned by the Queen to the House of Lords.

The main functions of Parliament are: to pass laws; to provide, by voting for taxation, the means of carrying on the work of government; to examine government policy and administration, including proposals for expenditure; and to debate the major issues of the day.

A Parliament has a maximum duration of five years, but in practice general elections are usually held before the end of this term. The life of a Parliament is divided into sessions. Each usually lasts for one year—normally beginning and ending in October or November. There are "adjournments" at night, at weekends, at Christmas, Easter and the late Spring Bank Holiday, and during a long summer break usually starting in late July.

The Sovereign formally summons and dissolves Parliament and generally opens each new annual session with a speech from the throne.

There are two tiers of local authority throughout England and Wales: counties and the smaller districts. At present England and Wales are divided into 53 counties, sub-divided into 369 districts. All the districts and 47 of the counties—the "non-metropolitan" counties—have locally elected councils. In the six metropolitan counties there are 36 district councils; there are no county councils.

When the Greater London Council was abolished in 1986 the various areas of responsibility of the former council were transferred to the London boroughs and government departments. Greater London is divided into 32 boroughs and the City of London, each of which has a council responsible for local government in its area.

On the mainland of Scotland, local government is at present on a two-tier basis: nine regions are divided into 53 districts, each of which has an elected council. Single-tier authorities were introduced for the three island areas (the Orkneys, the Shetlands and the Western Isles).

In Northern Ireland 26 district councils are responsible for local environmental and certain other services.

The local authorities run many of the public services. County councils provide large-scale services, while district councils are responsible for the more local ones. At present in England, county councils are responsible for strategic planning, transport planning, highways, traffic regulation, education, consumer protection, refuse disposal, police, the fire service, libraries and personal social services. District councils are responsible for environmental health, housing and refuse collection. In carrying out their duties, local authorities must act in accordance with, and within the limits of, powers conferred on them by Parliament; they are also subject to a certain amount of supervision by the central Government. Nevertheless, they remain independent bodies, and discharge their responsibilities in their own right. They also appoint and control their own staff.

Local government capital expenditure is financed primarily by borrowing and from capital receipts from the disposal of land and buildings. Local authorities in Great Britain raise revenue through the council tax.

## ▶ A Short Story ◀

### Commonwealth

Commonwealth is a traditional English term for a political community founded for the common good. Historically it has sometimes been synonymous with "republic."

The noun "commonwealth," meaning "public welfare general good or advantage" dates from the 15th century. Originally a phrase (the commonwealth or the common weal—echoed in the modern synonym "public weal") it comes from the old meaning of "wealth," which is "well-being," and is itself a loose translation of the Latin "res publica" (republic). The term literally meant "common well-being." In the 17th century, the definition of "commonwealth" expanded from its original sense of "public welfare" or "commonweal" to mean "a state in which the supreme power is vested in the people; a republic or democratic state." "Better things were done, and better managed... under a Commonwealth than under a King." Pepys, *Diary* (1667)

The term evolved to become a title to a number of political entities. Three countries—Australia, the Bahamas, and Dominica—have the official title "Commonwealth," as do four U.S. states and two U.S. territories. More recently, the term has been used to name some fraternal associations of nations, most notably the Commonwealth of Nations, an organization primarily of former territories of the British Empire, which is often referred to as simply "the Commonwealth."

## ▪▪▪ *Exercises* ▪▪▪

【Fill in the Blanks】

1. The _____ is the oldest institution of government, going back to at least the 9th century.

2. The term "parliament" originally meant a meeting for parley or _____.

3. In 1689, Parliament passed _____ to ensure that the king would never be able to ignore Parliament.

4. The Gentleman Usher of the Black Rod, is usually known as _____.

5. Life peers should be nominated by _____ and appointed by _____.

【Multiple Choices】

1. The Sovereign's coronation usually takes place at _____ in London.
   A. Westminster
   B. Yorkshire
   C. Bradford
   D. Westminster Abbey

2. Under whose reign was the *Bill of Rights* passed?
   A. James Ⅱ.
   B. William of Orange.
   C. Oliver Cromwell.
   D. George Ⅰ.

3. It is in the _____ that the ultimate authority for law-making resides.
   A. Cabinet
   B. House of Lords
   C. House of Commons
   D. Parliament

4. _____ serves as the role of the speaker in the House of Lords.
   A. Lord of Treasury
   B. Civil Servants
   C. Black Rod
   D. Lord chancellor

5. The leader of the Party with the largest number of votes in the General Election becomes _____. He or she is invited by the Queen to form a Government.
   A. the Prime Minister
   B. Lord chancellor
   C. Archbishop
   D. Judge

【Discussion】

1. What is a constitutional monarchy? When did it begin in Britain?

2. What is the role of the monarchy in the British government?

3. What are the main functions of Parliament?

# Unit 5

# Law

Britain was the first country to become a parliamentary democracy, but it has never worked out a single document containing its Constitution. That's why people say the United Kingdom has no written Constitution. As a matter of fact, Britain has its Constitution, but it is embodied in a number of separate laws passed by Parliament.

Britain's legal system is comprised of four elements: acts of Parliament, common law, equity law, and European Community legislation. They are all considered to have the binding force of a written constitution. Parliament can pass any law that is necessary and proper for the nation.

Common law came into being after the Norman Conquest in 1066. After the Normans conquered England, the Anglo-Norman kings used to send their judges on a tour all over the country to hear cases and punish offenders. There was no law to tell them how to deal with specific cases. The king's judges then made their decisions by relying on the traditions and conventions of the Anglo-Saxons. In doing so, they brought the various local practices into a single body of legal principles which were to be followed. Their verdicts in dealing with specific cases have been regarded as precedents by the English law courts and these precedents make up English common law.

Equity law might be regarded as a supplementary means used to deal with cases not covered by common law. When cases cannot be solved by using common law, petitions might be made to the king's Chancellor. These cases are usually concerned with moral problems or civil disputes, such as various kinds of contracts and debts. Judgments will be made according to the principle of equity.

As a member state of the European Community, the United Kingdom now abides by European Community legislation, which supersedes Britain's legislation.

There is no ministry of justice in the United Kingdom. Central responsibility lies with the Lord Chancellor, the Home Secretary and the Attorney General.

In England and Wales, lay magistrates are appointed on behalf of the Crown by the Lord Chancellor who is advised by committees in each county. In the Duchy of Lancaster, appointments are made by the Chancellor of the Duchy of Lancaster, a Cabinet minister. As far as the judges are concerned, appointments to the Circuit Bench and more senior judicial appointments are made by the Crown on the advice of ministers. The Lord Chancellor recommends the High Court and circuit judges, the recorders and the 76 metropolitan and stipendiary magistrates. The highest judicial appointments are made by the Queen on the advice of the Prime Minister.

In Scotland, the Secretary of State recommends the appointment of all judges other than the most senior one, and appoints the staff of the High Court of Justiciary and the Court of Session.

In Northern Ireland, court administration is the responsibility of the Lord Chancellor, while the Northern Ireland Office, under the Secretary of State, deals with policy and legislation concerning criminal law, the police and the penal system.

The chief aims of the penal system are to deter the potential lawbreaker, and to reform the convicted offender. Except for murder and certain rare offences, for which there are fixed penalties, the courts have power to vary the sentence within prescribed maxima in the light of the circumstances of the offence and the offender.

In England and Wales a Magistrates' court cannot impose a term of more than 6 months' imprisonment for an individual offence tried summarily. It can impose consecutive sentences for "either way" offences, subject to an overall maximum of 12 months' imprisonment. The Crown Court may impose a custodial sentence for any term up to life.

In Scotland in trials on indictment the High Court of Justiciary may impose a sentence of imprisonment for any term up to life, and the sheriff court any term up to three years. In summary cases, the sheriff or stipendiary magistrate may normally impose up to 3 months' imprisonment or 6 months' for some repeated offences. The district court can impose a maximum term of imprisonment of 60 days.

In Northern Ireland the position is generally the same as for England and Wales. A magistrates' court, however, cannot commit an offender for sentencing at the Crown Court if it has tried the case.

Capital punishment (a sentence of death) for murder has been abolished in the UK, though proposals for its reinstatement are regularly debated by Parliament, and it remains the penalty for treason and piracy.

About 80 per cent of offenders are punished with a fine. There is no limit to the fine which the Crown Court (and High Court of Justiciary in Scotland) may impose on indictment. The maximum fine that can be imposed by a magistrates' court in England and Wales is £5,000, although many summary offences carry lower maxima.

A court probation order can last between 6 months and 3 years; if the offender fails to comply with the order or commits another offence while on probation, he or she can be brought before the court again. A probation order can be combined with a community service order or a life.

The Prison Service in England and Wales and the Scottish Prison Service became executive agencies in April, 1993. There are about 130 prison establishments in England and Wales and some 20 in Scotland, many of which were built in the 19th century. In Northern Ireland there are 4 prisons and a young offenders' centre. Four of these establishments have been built since 1972. Training courses, educational schemes, medical services and welfare services are provided in all prisons; after-care for discharged prisoners operates throughout the United Kingdom.

In England and Wales young people aged 18–20 (16–21 in Scotland) serve custodial sentences in a young offender institution. In Northern Ireland offenders aged between 16 and 24 who receive custodial sentences of less than three years serve them in a young offenders' centre.

# ▶ A Short Story ◀

## The Lord Chancellor

The Lord Chancellor, formally the Lord High Chancellor of Great Britain, is a senior functionary in the government of the United Kingdom. They are appointed by the Sovereign on the advice of the Prime Minister. The Lord Chancellor is the second highest ranking of the Great Officers of State, ranking after only the Lord High Steward. Prior to the Union there were separate Lord Chancellors for England and Wales, for Scotland, and for Ireland.

The Lord Chancellor is a member of the Cabinet and, by law, is responsible for the efficient functioning and independence of the courts. In 2007 there were a number of changes to the legal system and to the office of the Lord Chancellor. Formerly, the Lord Chancellor was also the presiding officer of the House of Lords, the head of the judiciary in England and Wales, and the presiding judge of the Chancery Division of the High Court of Justice, but the *Constitutional Reform Act 2005* transferred these roles to the Lord Speaker, the Lord Chief Justice, and the Chancellor of the High Court respectively. The current Lord Chancellor is David Lidington, who is also the Secretary of State for Justice.

One of the Lord Chancellor's responsibilities is to act as the custodian of the Great Seal of the Realm. A Lord Keeper of the Great Seal may be appointed instead of a Lord Chancellor. The two offices entail exactly the same duties; the only distinction is in the mode of appointment. Furthermore, the office of Lord Chancellor may be exercised by a committee of individuals known as Lords Commissioners of the Great Seal, usually when there is a delay between an outgoing Chancellor and their replacement. The seal is then said to be "in commission." Since the 19th century, however, only Lord Chancellors have been appointed, the other offices having fallen into disuse.

## ••• Exercises •••

【Fill in the Blanks】

1. All criminal trials are held in _____ court.

2. In criminal trials by jury, the _____ passes sentence but the _____
   decides the issuer of guilt or innocence.

3. Magistrates' Courts which try _____ and _____ offences.

4. A feature common to all systems of law in the United Kingdom is
   that _____.

5. London's Metropolitan Police Force is directly under the control of
   the _____.

【Multiple Choices】

1. The jury system has been established in England since the time of
   King _____.
     A. Tudor        B. Henry II        C. Henry III        D. Charles I

2. Capital punishment has been abolished in _____ and _____.
     A. Scotland                  B. Wales
     C. the UK                  D. Northern Ireland

3. There are _____ police forces in England and Wales.
     A. 8        B. 33        C. 44        D. 43

4. _____ is a supplementary means to deal with cased not covered by
   common law.
     A. Equity law      B. Statutes      C. Unwritten law    D. Civil law

5. _____ is the ultimate court of appeal in civil cases throughout the UK.
     A. The House of Commons      B. The High Court
     C. Criminal Courts                D. The House of Lords

【Discussion】

Why do the criminal convicts like to be tried first before the magistrates'
courts?

## Unit 6

# Economy

Britain is the oldest industrial country in the world. The Industrial Revolution took place first in this country. Two centuries ago, Britain was known as the factory of the world. Many goods were manufactured in Britain and then sold all over the world. At that time the British economy was among the strongest in the world. Its standard of living was much higher than that of its European neighbors. However, today things are quite different. Soon after the Second World War, Britain not only gave up its economic hegemony but also suffered a deep loss of its position of industrial leadership. Its per capita GDP had been overtaken by the United States in 1900, by France and West Germany in 1950 and by Italy in 1960. Between 1950 and 1973, Britain's GDP grew at an average annual rate of 3.0%. This was lower than that of most of its trading partners. Growth was hampered by chronic balance of payments deficits. A country's balance of payments is the difference between the money from exports and the cost of imports and a country is running a balance of payments deficit when the country imports more goods and services than it exports. Britain has been running balance of payments deficits for many decades. As a result the British pound has fallen to its lowest level. Britain is no longer able to match the growth rates of other industrialized countries. The term "British disease" is now often used to characterize Britain's economic decline.

The evolution of the British economy since the Second World War falls into to following three periods:

The Second World War devastated Europe. The Britain economy suffered a great deal from the war, but it suffered less direct war damage than other

European countries and Japan. With help from the United States, the British economy quickly recovered. The consumer demand checked by the war soon became an important factor in contributing to the development of the economy. By the end of 1947, the British economy had returned to its pre-war levels. In 1950 Britain's GDP and its foreign trade ranked second (only after the U.S.) and its per capita income third in the world.

The British economy in this period is characterized by slow but steady growth, low unemployment and great material prosperity with rising standards of question of full employment to be the outstanding post-war economic problem. The economic policy it pursued was based on the theory of John M. Keynes. He suggested that the government should use fiscal and monetary policy to fine-tune aggregate demand to achieve full employment, while using prices and incomes policies to suppress inflation at source. High consumption and low investment which characterized this policy also brought about some problems. One of them was high labor cost, which in turn led to Britain's low competitiveness in international market. Although the British economy developed steadily in the 1950s and 1960s, it still lagged behind other industrialized. In the period of 1953-1963, Britain's average annual growth was 2.6% while the growth rate for the whole capitalist world was 5.6%, France was 4.6% and West Germany was 7.1%, in the 1950s Britain's industrial growth rate was only half of that of France.

Towards the end of the 1960s the rate of inflation began to rise. This further eroded business confidence and competitiveness. The end of 1973 witnessed the first oil shock. As a result the cost of oil imports skyrocketed. The rate of inflation rose to 9.1% in 1973 and to 16% in 1974. To combat high inflation, restrictive fiscal policies were adopted, which reduced growth. Between 1973 and 1979, GDP growth averaged 1.4% per year and the rate of inflation 15.6%. The second oil shock in 1977 caused inflation to rise still further. It reached a rate of 22% in 1980. In the 1970s among the developed countries Britain maintained the lowest growth rate and the highest inflation rate. In some years of the period Britain even had a minus growth and the trade deficits were the highest among the Western countries.

In March, 1979, the Conservative Party under the leadership of Mrs. Thatcher won the election. The new government adopted an economic programme known as Medium-term Financial Strategy, which in many ways represented a break with that of its predecessors. The new economic programme was based on the theory of the new classical school of thought. It turned "Keynesianism" on its head. Privatization, deregulation and market liberalization replaced prices and incomes control and state interventionism. Unlike the earlier Keynesian approach the new approach placed emphasis on improving the long-run supply-side performance of the economy.

The immediate effect of this approach was a deep recession in 1980–1981, with the GDP falling by a total of 2.6% in two years. By the end of 1980, unemployment reached a post-war record of over a million. Paradoxically, the British pound rose to a seven-year high of $2.45. Manufacturing competitiveness suffered from the high value of the pound. Output in the manufacturing sector fell by 14.2% in 1980–1981. However, by 1982 the downswing in world commodity prices together with the government's anti-inflationary policies led to dramatic falls in the rate of inflation to 8.6% in 1982 and to 5% in 1983. Between 1981and 1987 the GDP growth rate averaged 2.7%. Meanwhile Britain had become a sizable oil exporter and the economy had become more integrated with the global economy as well as with the EC economy.

An outstanding feature of the economic recovery in the 1980s was its length. By 1988 the recovery had lasted seven years. The previous two cycles lasted only two and four years. Another feature was the improved financial position of the government, with stronger current account of the balance of payments. An important factor in the recovery was the surge in labor productivity. In the 1980s only Japan recorded higher productivity figured than Britain.

In the 1980s Britain became a net exporter of oil. The oil sector made a substantial contribution to the current account. Oil exports peaked in 1984, when they accounted for about 16% of total exports of goods and services. The British economy in the 1980s developed quite significantly. The Thatcher programme was successful to some extent. Thatcher tried to cure the "British disease" by applying monetarism and encouraging the market-directed economy but she failed. By 1989 inflation caused by over-heated economy had risen to 8.3%. In April, 1990, it reached 9.4%. The balance of payments worsened again. In 1989, the visible trade deficit was 23.1 billion. There appeared a minus growth rate of 0.5% and 0.7% in the first two months of 1990. The new economic problems finally brought down the Conservative government headed by Thatcher. In November, 1990, she resigned as Prime Minister, bringing to an end one of the most remarkable periods in the British economy.

▚ *A Short Story* ▚

## Lady Thatcher

　Margaret Hilda Thatcher (October 13th, 1925–April 8th, 2013) was a British stateswoman who was Prime Minister of the United Kingdom from 1979 to 1990 and Leader of the Conservative Party from 1975 to 1990. She was the longest-serving British Prime Minister of the 20th century, and the first woman to have held the office. A Soviet journalist dubbed her "The Iron Lady," a nickname that came to be associated with her uncompromising politics and leadership style. As Prime Minister, she implemented policies that have come to be known as Thatcherism.

　A research chemist before becoming a barrister, Thatcher was elected Member of Parliament for Finchley in 1959. Edward Heath appointed her Secretary of State for Education and Science in his Conservative government. In 1975, Thatcher defeated Heath in the Conservative Party leadership election to become Leader of the Opposition and became the first woman to lead a major political party in the United Kingdom. She became Prime Minister after winning the 1979 general election.

　On moving into 10 Downing Street, Thatcher introduced a series of political and economic initiatives intended to reverse high unemployment and Britain's struggles in the wake of the Winter of Discontent and an ongoing recession. Her political philosophy and economic policies emphasized deregulation (particularly of the financial sector), flexible labour markets, the privatisation of state-owned companies, and reducing the power and influence of trade unions. Thatcher's popularity during her first years in office waned amid recession and increasing unemployment, until victory in the 1982 Falklands War and the recovering economy brought a resurgence of support, resulting in her decisive re-election in 1983. She survived an assassination attempt in 1984.

Thatcher was re-elected for a third term in 1987. During this period her support for a Community Charge (referred to as the "poll tax") was widely unpopular, and her views on the European Community were not shared by others in her Cabinet. She resigned as Prime Minister and party leader in November, 1990, after Michael Heseltine launched a challenge to her leadership. After retiring from the Commons in 1992, she was given a life peerage as Baroness Thatcher (of Kesteven in the County of Lincolnshire) which entitled her to sit in the House of Lords. In 2013, she died of a stroke in London at the age of 87. Always a controversial figure, she has nonetheless been lauded as one of the greatest, most influential and widest-known politicians in British history, even as arguments over Thatcherism persist.

## ▬▬ Exercises ▬▬

【Fill in the Blanks】

1. _____ is one of the busiest share-dealing centers in the world.

2. The British economy _____ in the 1970s and _____ in the 1980s.

3. In recent years, Britain is second only to the U.S. as a destination for _____ investment.

4. Today British coal mining is called a "_____" industry.

5. Traditionally Britain has had a deficit on visible trade and a _____ on invisible trade.

【Multiple Choices】

1. The evolution of the British economy since the Second World War falls into

_____ periods.

    A. two          B. three         C. four         D. five

2. An outstanding feature of the economic recovery in 1980s was its _____.

    A. length        B. time           C. effect        D. rate

3. In the 1980s Britain became a net exporter of _____, with production peaking in 1984.

    A. coal           B. gas            C. steel         D. oil

4. Britain became a world leader in ship building during the middle of the _____ century.

    A. 17th          B. 18th          C. 19th         D. 20th

5. About half of Britain's foreign trade is with the member countries of _____.

    A. the ED       B. the UN       C. the EC       D. the GDP

【Discussion】

1. What are the three periods as far as the evolution of the British economy is concerned?

2. What measures did the Thatcher government take to improve the nation's economy?

# Unit 7

# Education

Education in the United Kingdom is a devolved matter with each of the countries of the United Kingdom having separate systems under separate governments: the UK Government is directly responsible for England; whilst the Scottish Government, the Welsh Government and the Northern Ireland Executive are responsible for Scotland, Wales and Northern Ireland, respectively. English, Welsh and Northern Irish students tend to sit a small number of more advanced examinations and Scottish students tend to sit a larger number of less advanced examinations. In England and Wales, the EYFS (Early Years Foundation Stage) is applicable to children aged 5 and below, and the national curriculum is applicable to children aged above 5.

In each country there are five stages of education: early years, primary, secondary, further education (FE) and higher education (HE). The law states that full time education is compulsory for all children between the ages of 5 (4 in Northern Ireland) and 16. In England, compulsory education or training has been extended to 18 for those born on or after September 1st, 1997. This full-time education does not need to be at a school and a number of parents choose to home educate. Before they reach compulsory school age, children can be educated at nursery if parents wish though there is only limited government funding for such places. Further Education is non-compulsory, and covers non-advanced education which can be taken at further (including tertiary) education colleges and Higher Education Institutions (HEIs).

In education in the United Kingdom, a grammar school is a secondary school attended by pupils aged 11 to 18 to which entry is controlled by means of an academically selective process consisting, largely or exclusively, of a written examination. After leaving a grammar school, as with any other secondary school, a student may go into further education at a college or university. To understand grammar schools in the UK, some history is needed. After World War II, the government reorganized the secondary schools into two basic types: secondary moderns were intended for children who would be going into a trade and concentrated on the basics plus practical skills; grammar schools were intended for children who would be going on to higher education and concentrated on the classics, science, etc. This system lasted until the 1960s, at which point changes in the political climate led to the general acceptance that this was a discriminatory system which was not getting the best out of all children. This was partly because some authorities tended to priorities their budgets on the grammar schools, damaging the education prospects of children attending secondary moderns. The decision was taken to switch to a single type of school designed to give every child a complete education. That is why this new type of school is called a comprehensive school. However the timetable of the changeover was left to the local authorities, some of whom were very resistant to the whole idea and thus dragged their feet for as long as possible. The result is that there is now a mixture. Most authorities run a proper comprehensive system, a few run essentially the old system of secondary moderns and grammar schools (except the secondary moderns are now called "comprehensives"). Some run comprehensive schools alongside one or two remaining grammar schools.

The fifth stage, Higher Education, is study beyond A levels or BTECs (and their equivalent) which, for most full-time students, takes place in universities and other Higher Education institutions and colleges. The UK's higher education system is world famous. Universities in the UK have a role in every aspect of UK life—from shaping government policy to working with artists and scientists. Therefore, UK qualifications are highly respected by employers and academics worldwide. The UK teaching system is designed to encourage students to ask questions, debate and come up with their own ideas. UK universities and colleges combine practical learning with lectures and seminars and embrace innovative teaching methods and high-tech learning environments. There is a wide range of opportunities to gain practical experience. Many courses have options for work placements and internships that count towards the degree. Many offer the chance to gain professional accreditation, too. However, the education system differs slightly in the four countries that make up the UK. Scottish higher education degrees tend to last four years rather than three years (more common in England, Wales and Northern Ireland). Many students in Scotland also move into higher education at the age of 17, rather than 18, as in other parts of the UK. Higher education includes both the teaching and the research activities of universities, and within the realm of teaching, it includes both the undergraduate level (sometimes referred to as tertiary education ) and the graduate (or postgraduate ) level (sometimes referred to as quaternary education). Higher education differs from other forms of post-secondary education such as vocational education. However, most professional education is included within higher education, and many postgraduate qualifications are strongly vocationally or professionally oriented, for example in disciplines such as law and medicine.

The National Curriculum (NC), established in 1988, provides a framework for education in England and Wales between the ages of 5 and 18. Though the National Curriculum is not compulsory it is followed by most state schools, but some private schools, academies, free schools and home educators design their own curricula.

Funding for UK schools will change to a national formula in 2018, with some schools likely to gain from the new formula and others likely to lose. The National Audit Office (NAO) claims that funding will be cut by 8%. Opponents fear class sizes will increase, schools will be less able to buy basic equipment and children's life chances will be damaged. With supersized primary schools, large class sizes and the squeeze on primary school places, some parents are choosing to educate their children at home for part of the week although none of the parents wants to commit themselves to full-time home education, and, in any case, they are supporters of comprehensive education. Grammar schools also face problems, many claim their funding will be cut. Some are considering asking parents for financial contributions. It is very difficult to obtain funding for postgraduate study in the UK. There are a few scholarships for master's courses, but these are rare and dependent on the course and class of undergraduate degree obtained. Most master's students are self-funded. Funding is available for some Ph.D. courses. There is more funding available to those in the sciences than in other disciplines.

Some 93% of children between the ages of 3 and 18 are in education in state-funded schools without charge (other than for activities such as swimming, theatre visits and field trips for which a voluntary payment can be requested, and limited charges at state-funded boarding schools Primary and Secondary education can also be charged for, if a fee-paying school is attended by the child in question). The costs for a normal education in the United Kingdom are as follows:

Primary: No Charge.

Secondary: No Charge.

Further (Secondary) Education in either a sixth form or college: No Charge if under 19 in that particular academic year or on a low income.

Higher / Tertiary Education (University): A tuition fee per year (varies from £1,000 to £9,000).

A public school, in common British usage, is a school usually prestigious and historic, which charges fees, does not restrict admissions, and is financed by bodies other than the state, commonly as a private charitable trust. Often but not always they are boarding schools. Confusingly to a non-native English speaker a public school is actually a private school! In British usage, a government-run school (which would be called a "public school" in other areas, such as the United States ) is called a state school in the UK. Public schools played an important role in the development of the Victorian social elite. Under a number of forward-looking headmasters leading public schools developed a curriculum based heavily on classics and physical activity for boys and young men of the upper and upper middle classes. They were schools for the gentlemanly elite of Victorian politics, armed forces and colonial government. Often successful businessmen would send their sons to public school as a mark of participation in the elite. Today most public schools are highly selective on academic grounds, as well as financial grounds (ability to pay high fees) and social grounds (often a family connection to the school is very desirable in admissions).

## ▶ A Short Story ◀

### University of Cambridge

The University of Cambridge (informally Cambridge University) is a collegiate public research university in Cambridge, England. Founded in 1209 and granted a royal charter by King Henry III in 1231, Cambridge is the second-oldest university in the English-speaking world and the world's fourth-oldest surviving university. The university grew out of an association of scholars who left the University of Oxford after a dispute with the townspeople. The two medieval universities share many common features and are often referred to jointly as "Oxbridge."

Cambridge is formed from a variety of institutions which include 31 constituent colleges and over 100 academic departments organised into six schools. Cambridge University Press, a department of the university, is the world's oldest publishing house and the second-largest university press in the world. The university also operates eight cultural and scientific museums, including the Fitzwilliam Museum, as well as a botanic garden. Cambridge's libraries hold a total of around 15 million books, eight million of which are in Cambridge University Library, a legal deposit library.

In the year ended July 31st, 2016, the university had a total income of £1.64 billion, of which £462 million was from research grants and contracts. The central university and colleges have a combined endowment of around £5.89 billion, the largest of any university outside the United States. The university is closely linked with the development of the high-tech business cluster known as "Silicon Fen". It is a member of numerous associations and forms part of the "golden triangle" of leading English universities and Cambridge University Health Partners, an academic health science centre.

As of September 2017, Cambridge is ranked the world's second best university by the World University Rankings, the world's fourth best university by three other ranking tables, and no other institution in the world ranks in the top 10 for as many subjects. The university has educated many notable alumni, including eminent mathematicians, scientists, politicians, lawyers, philosophers, writers, actors and foreign Heads of State. Ninety-five Nobel laureates, fifteen British prime ministers and ten Fields medalists have been affiliated with Cambridge as students, faculty or alumni.

## ▪▪▪ *Exercises* ▪▪▪

【Fill in the Blanks】

1. The two oldest universities in Britain are _____ and _____.

2. Two famous public schools mentioned in the text are _____ and _____.

3. Students attend _____ schools from the age of 11 up to around the age of 19.

4. Parents can choose between sending their children to state schools or _____ schools.

5. In Britain, people can go to the _____ without having any formal educational qualifications.

【Multiple Choices】

1. In Britain, children from the age of 5 to 16 _____.

   A. can legally receive partly free education

   B. can legally receive completely free education

   C. can not receive free education at all

   D. can not receive free education if their parents are rich

2. In Britain, the great majority of parents send their children to _____.

   A. private schools　　　　　　　　B. independent schools

   C. state schools　　　　　　　　　D. public schools

3. Which of the following is a privately funded university in Britain?

   A. The University of Cambridge.

B. The University of Oxford.

C. The University of Edinburgh.

D. The University of Buckingham.

4. Which of the following is not a characteristic of the Open University?

    A. It's open to everybody.

    B. It requires no formal educational qualifications.

    C. No university degree is awarded.

    D. University courses are followed through TV, radio, correspondence, etc.

5. Which of the following schools would admit children without reference to their academic abilities?

    A. Comprehensive schools.              B. Secondary schools.

    C. Independent schools.                D. Grammar schools.

【Discussion】

1. How many stages of education are there in the UK?

2. What is encouraged in the British Higher Education teaching system?

3. Is the concept of British public school similar to that of Chinese public school? How is British public school funded?

## Unit 8

# Literature

British literature is literature in the English language from the United Kingdom, Isle of Man, and Channel Islands. Anglo-Saxon (Old English) literature is included, and there is some discussion of Latin and Anglo-Norman literature, where literature in these languages relate to the early development of the English language and literature. There is also some brief discussion of major figures who wrote in Scots, but the main discussion is in the various Scottish literature articles.

Irish writers have played an important part in the development of literature in England and Scotland, but though the whole of Ireland was politically part of the United Kingdom between January 1801 and December 1922, it can be controversial to describe Irish literature as British. For some this includes works by authors from Northern Ireland.

The nature of British identity has changed over time. The island that contains, England, Scotland, and Wales, has been known as Britain from the time of the Roman Pliny the Elder (AD 23-79). Though the original inhabitants spoke mainly various Celtic languages, English as the national language had its beginnings with the Anglo-Saxon invasion of 450 A.D.

The various constituent parts of the present United Kingdom joined at different times. Wales was annexed by the Kingdom of England under the *Acts of Union* of 1536 and 1542. However, it was not until 1707 with a treaty between England and Scotland that the Kingdom of Great Britain came into existence. This merged in January 1801 with the Kingdom of Ireland to form the United Kingdom of Great Britain and Ireland. Until fairly recent times the original Celtic languages continued to be spoken in Scotland, Wales,

Cornwall, and Ireland, and still survive, especially in parts of Wales.

Subsequently, the impact of Irish nationalism led to the partition of the island of Ireland in 1921, which means that literature of the Republic of Ireland is not British, although literature from Northern Ireland is both Irish and British.

Works written in the English language by Welsh writers, especially if their subject matter relates to Wales, have been recognized as a distinctive entity since the twentieth-century. The need for a separate identity for this kind of writing arose because of the parallel development of modern Welsh-language literature.

Because Britain was a colonial power, the use of English spread through the world, and from the nineteenth-century in the United States, and later in other former colonies. Major writers in English, including Nobel laureates, began to appear beyond the boundaries of Britain and Ireland.

### Old English literature: circa. 658–1100

Old English literature, or Anglo-Saxon literature, encompasses the surviving literature written in Old English in Anglo-Saxon England, in the period after the settlement of the Saxons and other Germanic tribes in England (Jutes and the Angles) circa 450, after the withdrawal of the Romans, and "ending soon after the Norman Conquest" in 1066; that is, circa 1100–1150. These works include genres such as epic poetry, hagiography, sermons, Bible translations, legal works, chronicles, riddles, and others. In all there are about 400 surviving manuscripts from this period.

Nearly all Anglo-Saxon authors are anonymous: twelve are known by name from Medieval sources, but only four of those are known by their vernacular works with any certainty: Cædmon, Bede, Alfred the Great, and Cynewulf. Cædmon is the earliest English poet whose name is known. Cædmon's only known surviving work is *Cædmon's Hymn*, which probably dates back to the late 7th century.

### Middle English literature: 1066–1485

Sir Bedivere cast King Arthur's sword Excalibur back to the Lady of the Lake. The Arthurian Cycle has influenced British literature across languages and down the centuries. The linguistic diversity of the islands in the medieval period contributed to a rich variety of artistic production, and made British literature distinctive and innovative.

In this period, works were still written in Latin and included Gerald of Wales's late-12th-century book on his beloved Wales, *Itinerarium Cambriae*, and following the Norman Conquest of 1066, Anglo-Norman literature developed in the Anglo-Norman realm introducing literary trends from Continental Europe. However, the indigenous development of Anglo-Norman literature was precocious in comparison to continental European literature.

Interest in King Arthur continued in 15th century with Sir Thomas Malory's *Le Morte d'Arthur* (1485), a popular and influential compilation of some French and English Arthurian romances. It was among the earliest books printed in England by Caxton.

In the later medieval period a new form of English now known as Middle English evolved. This is the earliest form which is comprehensible to modern readers and listeners, though not easily. Middle English Bible translations, notably *Wycliffe's Bible*, helped to establish English as a literary language. *Wycliffe's Bible* is the name now given to a group of Bible translations into Middle English that were made under the direction of, or at the instigation of, John Wycliffe. They appeared over a period from approximately 1382 to 1395.

Women writers were also active, such as Marie de France in the 12th century and Julian of Norwich in the early 14th century. Julian's *Revelations of Divine Love* (circa 1393) is believed to be the first published book written by a woman in the English language. Margery Kempe (circa 1373−after 1438) is known for writing *The Book of Margery Kempe*, a work considered by some to be the first autobiography in the English language.

### The Renaissance: 1485-1660

The English Renaissance and the Renaissance in Scotland date from the late 15th century to the early 17th century. Italian literary influences arrived in Britain: the sonnet form was introduced into English by Thomas Wyatt in the early 16th century, and developed by Henry Howard, Earl of Surrey, (1516/1517−1547), who also introduced blank verse into England, with his translation of Virgil's Aeneid in c. 1540.

The spread of printing affected the transmission of literature across Britain and Ireland. The first book printed in English, William Caxton's own translation of *Recuyell of the Historyes of Troye*, was printed abroad in 1473, to be followed by the establishment of the first printing press in England in 1474.

Latin continued in use as a language of learning long after the Reformation had established the vernaculars as liturgical languages for the elites.

*Utopia* is a work of fiction and political philosophy by Thomas More (1478–1535) published in 1516. The book, written in Latin, is a frame narrative primarily depicting a fictional island society and its religious, social and political customs.

Shakespeare also popularized the English sonnet, which made significant changes to Petrarch's model. A collection of 154 by sonnets, dealing with themes such as the passage of time, love, beauty and mortality, were first published in a 1609 quarto.

Besides Shakespeare the major poets of the early 17th century included the metaphysical poets John Donne (1572–1631) and George Herbert (1593–1633). Influenced by continental Baroque, and taking as his subject matter both Christian mysticism and eroticism, Donne's metaphysical poetry uses unconventional or "unpoetic" figures, such as a compass or a mosquito, to reach surprise effects.

**Late Renaissance: 1625–1660**

The metaphysical poets continued writing in this period. Both John Donne and George Herbert died after 1625, but there was a second generation of metaphysical poets, consisting of Andrew Marvell (1621–1678), Thomas Traherne (1636 or 1637–1674) and Henry Vaughan (1622–1695). Their style was characterized by wit and metaphysical conceits—far-fetched or unusual similes or metaphors, such as in Andrew Marvell's comparison of the soul with a drop of dew, or Donne's description of the effects of absence on lovers to the action of a pair of compasses.

Another important group of poets at this time were the Cavalier poets. They were an important group of writers, who came from the classes that supported King Charles I during the Wars of the Three Kingdoms (1639–1651). (King Charles reigned from 1625 and was executed in 1649). The best known of the Cavalier poets are Robert Herrick, Richard Lovelace, Thomas Carew, and Sir John Suckling. They "were not a formal group, but all were influenced" by Ben Jonson. Most of the Cavalier poets were courtiers, with notable exceptions.

## Romanticism: 1798–1837

Romanticism was an artistic, literary, and intellectual movement that originated in Europe toward the end of the 18th century. Various dates are given for the Romantic period in British literature, but here the publishing of *Lyrical Ballads* in 1798 is taken as the beginning, and the crowning of Queen Victoria in 1837 as its end, even though, for example, William Wordsworth lived until 1850 and William Blake published before 1798. The writers of this period, however, "did not think of themselves as 'Romantics', " and the term "Romantics" was first used by critics of the Victorian period.

The Romantic period was one of the major social changes in England, because of the depopulation of the countryside and the rapid development of overcrowded industrial cities, which took place in the period roughly between 1785 and 1830. The movement of so many people in England was the result of two forces: the Agricultural Revolution, that involved the Enclosure of the land, drove workers off the land, and the Industrial Revolution which provided them employment, "in the factories and mills, operated by machines driven by steam-power." Indeed, Romanticism may be seen in part as a reaction to the Industrial Revolution, though it was also a revolt against aristocratic social and political norms of the Age of Enlightenment, as well a reaction against the scientific rationalization of nature. The French Revolution had an especially important influence on the political thinking of many of the Romantic poets.

The landscape is often prominent in the poetry of this period, so the Romantics, especially perhaps Wordsworth, are often described as "nature poets." However, the Romantic "nature poems" have a wider concern because they are usually meditations on "an emotional problem or personal crisis."

### The 20th-century literature

The year 1922 marked a significant change in the relationship between Great Britain and Ireland, with the setting up of the (predominantly Catholic) Irish Free State in most of Ireland, while the predominantly Protestant Northern Ireland remained part of the United Kingdom. This separation also leads to questions as to what extent Irish writing prior to 1922 should be treated as a colonial literature. There are also those who question whether the literature of Northern Ireland is Irish or British. Nationalist movements in Britain, especially in Wales and Scotland, also significantly influenced writers in the 20th and 21st centuries.

### The 21st century literature

Dame Hilary Mantel is a highly successful writer of historical novels winning the Booker Prize twice, for *Wolf Hall 2009* and *Bring Up the Bodies*. Julian Barnes (1946– ) is another prominent writer and he won the 2011 Man Booker Prize for his book *The Sense of an Ending*. The perceived success and promotion of genre fiction authors from Scotland provoked controversy in 2009 when James Kelman criticised, in a speech at the Edinburgh International Book Festival, the attention afforded to "upper middle-class young magicians" and "detective fiction" by the "Anglo-centric" Scottish literary establishment.

## ▶ A Short Story ◀

### William Shakespeare

William Shakespeare was an English poet, playwright, and actor, widely regarded as the greatest writer in the English language and the world's pre-eminent dramatist. He is often called England's national poet, and the "Bard of Avon." His extant works, including collaborations, consist of approximately 38 plays, 154 sonnets, two long narrative poems, and a few other verses, some of uncertain authorship. His plays have been translated into every major living language and are performed more often than those of any other playwright.

Shakespeare was born and brought up in Stratford-upon-Avon, Warwickshire. At the age of 18, he married Anne Hathaway, with whom he had three children: Susanna, and twins Hamnet and Judith. Sometime between 1585 and 1592, he began a successful career in London as an actor, writer, and part-owner of a playing company called the Lord Chamberlain's Men, later known as the King's Men. He appeared to have retired to Stratford around 1613, at age 49, where he died three years later. Few records of Shakespeare's private life survive, which has stimulated considerable speculation about such matters as his physical appearance, sexuality, religious beliefs, and whether the works attributed to him were written by others.

Shakespeare produced most of his known work between 1589 and 1613. His early plays were primarily comedies and histories, which are regarded as some of the best work ever produced in these genres. He then wrote mainly tragedies until about 1608, including *Hamlet*, *Othello*, *King Lear*, and *Macbeth*, considered some of the finest works in the English language. In his last phase, he wrote tragicomedies, also known as romances, and collaborated with other playwrights.

Many of his plays were published in editions of varying quality and accuracy during his lifetime. In 1623, however, John Heminges and Henry Condell, two friends and fellow actors of Shakespeare, published a more definitive text known as the *First Folio*, a posthumous collected edition of his dramatic works that included all but two of the plays now recognised as Shakespeare's. It was prefaced with a poem by Ben Jonson, in which Shakespeare is hailed, presciently, as "not of an age, but for all time."

In the 20th and 21st centuries, his works have been repeatedly adapted and rediscovered by new movements in scholarship and performance. His plays remain highly popular and are constantly studied, performed, and reinterpreted in diverse cultural and political contexts throughout the world.

## ▪▪▪ Exercises ▪▪▪

【Fill in the Blanks】

1. Name two of the tragedies written by Shakespeare: _____ and _____.

2. 20th-century literature can be broadly divided into two stylistic periods: _____ and _____.

3. The best-know novel by William Golding is titled _____.

4. *The Heart of Darkness* was written by _____; the author of the book *1984* was _____.

5. One of the oldest of the early "Old English" literary work is a long poem from Anglo Saxon times called _____.

【Multiple Choices】

1. Which literary form flourished in Elizabethan age more than any other forms of literature?

   A. Novel.　　　B. Essay.　　　C. Drama.　　　D. Poetry.

2. Among the following writer, who was not one of the great trio?

   A. Ben Johnson.　　　　　　　　B. William Shakespeare.

   C. Thomas Malory.　　　　　　　D. Ben Johnson.

3. Which of the following did not belong to Romanticism?

   A. Keats.　　　B. Shelley.　　　C. Wordsworth.　　　D. Defoe.

4. Which of the following tragedy is written by Shakespeare?

   A. *Doctor Faustus*.　　　　　　B. *Macbeth*.

   C. *Frankenstein*.　　　　　　　D. *The Tempest*.

5. Which of the following writers was not associated with Modernism?

   A. D. H. Lawrence.　　　　　　B. E. M. Forster.

   C. Charles Dickens.　　　　　　D. Virginia Woolf.

【Discussion】

1. What are some of the features of Romantic Literature?

2. What is Modernism and what is Postmodernism?

## Unit 9

# The Mass Media

As is known that with the development of technology, the influence of media has become far-reaching and profound as it not only informs people like it has been for centuries, but more importantly, shapes the way we perceive the world. In 2009, it was estimated that individuals viewed a mean of 3.75 hours of television per day and listened to 2.81 hours of radio. According to Curran, "contrary to the illusion that media only 'mediates' what goes on in the rest of the society, the media's representational power is one of the society's main forces in its own right." In this concentrated form, symbolic power (including media power) is better defined as a "power of constructing reality"—that is, social reality. To contest media power is to contest the way social reality itself is defined or named. Therefore, getting a handle of British media may bring a better understanding of British culture as a whole. Media of the United Kingdom consists of several different types of media including television, radio, newspaper, magazine as well as websites. In the United Kingdom, London dominates the media sector in the United Kingdom: national newspapers, television and radio are largely based there, notable centers including Fleet Street and BBC Broadcasting House.

Before getting to the media in the United Kingdom, however, it is worth noting the concept of freedom of expression. In the United Kingdom, freedom of expression is highly valued and protected as it is considered a universal human right. It is not the prerogative of the politician, nor is it the privilege of the journalists. In their day-to-day work, journalists are simply exercising every citizen's right to free speech.

A free press is fundamental to a democratic society. It seeks out and circulates news, information, ideas, comment and opinion and holds those in authority to account. The press provides the platform for a multiplicity of voices to be heard. At national, regional and local level, it is the public's watchdog, activist and guardian as well as educator, entertainer and contemporary chronicler.

Ofcom is the independent regulator and competition authority for the communication industries in the United Kingdom, including television. It requires that certain television and radio broadcasters fulfill certain requirements as part of their license to broadcast. All of the BBC's television and radio stations have a public service remit, including those that broadcast digitally.

*Specification of the Broadcast Code* took effect on July 25th, 2005, with the latest version being published October 2008. The Code itself is published on Ofcom's website, and provides a mandatory set of rules which broadcast programmers must comply with. The 10 main sections cover protection of under-eighteens, harm and offence, crime, religion, impartiality and accuracy, elections, fairness, privacy, sponsorship and commercial references. As stipulated in the *Communications Act 2003*, Ofcom enforces adherence to the Code. Failure for a broadcaster to comply with the Code results in warnings, fines, and potentially revocation of a broadcasting license.

Examining specific complaints by viewers or other bodies about programmers and sponsorship, Ofcom issues Broadcast Bulletins on a fortnightly basis which is accessible via its website. As an example, a bulletin from February 2009 has a complaint from the National Heart Forum over sponsorship of *The Simpsons* by Domino's Pizza on Sky1. Ofcom concluded this was in breach of the Broadcast Code, since it contravened an advertising restriction of food high in fat, salt or sugar. The results of the consultations are published by Ofcom, and inform the policies that Ofcom creates and enforces.

To get to know the British television sector, it is of importance to understand what PSB, i.e. public service broadcasting, stands for. In the United Kingdom, the term "public service broadcasting" refers to broadcasting intended for public benefit rather than to serve purely commercial interests. The United Kingdom has a diverse range of providers, the most prominent being the state-owned public service broadcaster, the British Broadcasting Corporation (BBC). The domestic services of the BBC are funded by the television licence. The international television broadcast services are operated by BBC Worldwide on a commercial subscription basis over cable and satellite services. The commercial operators rely on advertising for their revenue, and are run as commercial ventures, in contrast to the public service operators.

The United Kingdom print publishing sector, including books, server, directories and databases, journals, magazines and business media, newspapers and news agencies, has a combined turnover of around £20 billion and employs around 167,000 people. The print media sector is entirely regulating itself and there are no specific statutory rules regulating the print media.

Traditionally British newspapers have been divided into "quality", serious-minded newspapers (usually referred to as "broadsheets" because of their large size) and the more populist, "tabloid" varieties. In 2008, *The Sun* had the highest circulation of any daily newspaper in the United Kingdom at 3.1 million, approximately a quarter of the market. Its sister paper, *the News of the World*, had the highest circulation in the Sunday newspaper market, and traditionally focused on celebrity-led stories until its closure in 2011. *The Daily Telegraph*, a centre-right broadsheet paper, is the highest-selling of the "quality" newspapers. *The Guardian* is a more liberal "quality" broadsheet and the *Financial Times* is the main business newspaper, printed on distinctive salmon-pink broadsheet paper.

The *News International* phone hacking scandal is an ongoing controversy involving the *News of the World* and other British newspapers published by *News International*, a subsidiary of Murdoch's News Corporation. Employees of the newspaper were convicted of engaging in phone hacking, police bribery, and exercising improper influence in the pursuit of publishing stories. Advertiser boycotts contributed to the closure of the *News of the World* on

July 10th, ending 168 years of publication.

The Leveson inquiry is a judicial public inquiry into the culture, practices and ethics of the British press following the *News International* phone hacking scandal, chaired by Lord Justice Leveson, who was appointed in July 2011. A series of public hearings were held throughout 2011 and 2012. The Inquiry published the *Leveson Report* in November 2012, which reviewed the general culture and ethics of the British media, and made recommendations for a new, independent body to replace the existing Press Complaints Commission, which would be recognized by the state through new laws.

During the early 21st century, many newspapers saw a rapid decline in circulation. The sector's advertising revenues fell 15% during 2015 alone, with an estimate of a further 20% drop over the course of 2016. The decline of the newspaper industry has been linked to the rise of internet usage in Britain.

Radio in the United Kingdom is dominated by the BBC, which operates radio stations both in the United Kingdom and abroad. The BBC World Service radio network is broadcast in 33 languages globally. Domestically the BBC also operates ten national networks and over 40 local radio stations including services in Welsh. The most popular radio station by number of listeners is BBC Radio 2, closely followed by BBC Radio 4.

Rather than operating as independent entities, many commercial local radio stations are owned by large radio groups which broadcast a similar format to many areas. The largest operator of radio stations is Global Radio, owner of the major Heart and Galaxy radio brands. It also owns Classic FM and London's most popular commercial radio station, 95.8 Capital FM. Other owners are UTV Radio, with stations broadcasting in large city areas and Bauer Radio, holding radio in the North of England. There are also regional stations, like Real Radio and the Century Network, broadcasting in some main parts of England, Wales and Scotland and a number of licensed community radio stations, which broadcast to local audiences.

The United Kingdom has been involved with the Internet since it was created. The UK's country code top-level domain (ccTLD) is UK. The most visited "UK" website is the British version of Google, followed by Amazon, eBay and BBC Online.

## *A Short Story*

### BBC

The British Broadcasting Corporation (BBC) is a British public service broadcaster with its headquarters at Broadcasting House in London. The BBC is the world's oldest national broadcasting organisation and the largest broadcaster in the world by number of employees. It employs over 20,950 staff in total, 16,672 of whom are in public sector broadcasting. The total number of staff is 35, 402 when part-time, flexible, and fixed contract staff are included.

The BBC is established under a Royal Charter and operates under its Agreement with the Secretary of State for Culture, Media and Sport. Its work is funded principally by an annual television licence fee which is charged to all British households, companies, and organisations using any type of equipment to receive or record live television broadcasts and iPlayer catch-up. The fee is set by the British Government, agreed by Parliament, and used to fund the BBC's radio, TV, and online services covering the nations and regions of the UK. Since April 1st, 2014, it has also funded the BBC World Service (launched in 1932 as the BBC Empire Service), which broadcasts in 28 languages and provides comprehensive TV, radio, and online services in Arabic and Persian.

Around a quarter of BBC revenues comes from its commercial arm BBC Worldwide Ltd., which sells BBC programmes and services internationally and also distributes the BBC's international 24-hour English-language news services BBC World News, and from BBC. com, provided by BBC Global News Ltd.

*** *Exercises* ***

【Fill in the Blanks】

1. BBC is the abbreviation of the _____ _____ _____, using English and _____ other languages.

2. There are 4 British national channels, _____, _____, _____, and _____.

3. The _____ newspapers carry more serious and in-depth articles of particular political and social importance.

4. The BBC stands for _____.

5. _____ is regarded as the most left-wing newspaper in Britain.

【Multiple Choices】

1. Which of the following newspaper is a tabloid?

   A. *The News of the World*.     B. *East Enders*.

   C. *The Telegraph*.             D. None of the above.

2. Quality newspapers are directed at readers _____.

   A. who want news of a more entertaining character

   B. who care for mid-market

   C. who love music

   D. who want full information on a wide range of public matters

3. In Britain most advertising is carried _____.

   A. in newspapers                B. in magazines

   C. on television                D. on radio

4. How many newspapers are there in Britain?

   A. About 100.     B. About 1400.     C. About 150.     D. About 140.

5. Which of the following is the world's oldest national newspaper?

   A. *The Times*.                 B. *The Guardian*.

   C. *The Observer*.              D. *The Financial Times*.

【Discussion】

1. What are the five types of media in the United Kingdom?
2. What is the independent regulator and competition authority for the communication industries in the United Kingdom?
3. What is the largest radio operator in the United Kingdom?

## Unit 10

# Festivals and Public Holidays

The Christian festivals of the year are Christmas, Easter, and Whit Sunday.

Christmas Day, December 25th, celebrates the birth of Christ, and is the greatest of Christian festivals. Two important things, apart from its religious significance, help to set this festival apart from all others: the custom of giving gifts and the habit of spending it with the family.

In the present highly commercialized age we are reminded of Christmas many weeks before the event. In the shops the special Christmas displays appear and outside them are the special Christmas decorations. In the shopping centers of very large towns decorations are put up in the streets. In London thousands of people flock into the center of the town to see the decorations in Oxford Street, Regent Street, Piccadilly and elsewhere. The advertisements in the newspapers remind us incessantly that there are "only x more shopping days to Christmas." The post office vans are covered with brightly colored posters urging people to "Post Early for Christmas," for hundreds of millions of Christmas cards and millions of parcels are sent every year. Everywhere one turns, one is made aware that Christmas, which comes "but once a year," is coming once again.

Many people deplore what they consider the over-commercialization of a sacred holiday, but, underneath all the business activity, a great deal of genuine Christmas spirit is to be found. The custom of giving presents to one's family and friends is a very pleasant one as long as one remembers that it is the spirit behind the gift which matters most and not the gift itself. And how good it is at Christmas to return to the family home and meet parents, grandparents and as many aunts, uncles and cousins as can be accommodated. Without 21 century means of transport, many families would be denied the Christmas reunion.

At Christmas, the home is decorated with colorful paper chains, leaves of holly and mistletoe, and attractive greetings cards received through the post from friends. In the corner there may be a young fir tree standing in a large pot. This is the "Christmas tree," with its branches decorated with shining ornaments and colored lights, and sometimes hung with gifts.

On Christmas Eve, the traditional ritual of hanging up a stocking at the foot of the bed is performed by millions of excited children. They hope that Father Christmas (also called Santa Claus), a merry old man with a long white beard and a long red coat trimmed with white fur, will steal in to deliver presents they have asked for in the morning of the Christmas Day.

Christmas Day is spent quietly at home. The excitement of all the presents is hardly over before it is time for the traditional Christmas dinner: turkey, duck or chicken with rich fruity Christmas pudding afterwards. At tea-time the crackers are pulled. The evening is spent in games, merriment and more eating and drinking.

New Year's Day (January 1st) is part of Scottish "Hogmanay" (New Year's Eve) festival, which is more important than Christmas to Scots. Here the main celebration is on New Year's Eve, when in England as well as in Scotland, people stay up late, often at a party or a religious "watch-night service," to see the New Year in. As the clocks strike midnight between December 31st and January 1st, church bells start ringing joyfully, and people at their parties drink a toast to the New Year, wishing their friends happiness and prosperity. It is a Scottish tradition that the first person to cross the threshold of your house on New Year's Day should be dark-haired such a person brings luck for the coming year.

The only other national festival is Guy Fawkes Day. The origin of this festival lies in the Gunpowder Plot of 1605. In that year King James I was on the throne. Harsh measures had been taken against members of the Roman Catholic faith and certain Catholics plotted to blow up the Houses of

Parliament on November 5th, when the King was to open Parliament, of course, all the Members would be present. The plot was discovered, and one of the conspirators, Guy Fawkes, was arrested in the cellars of the House of Commons, where 36 barrels of gunpowder had been placed in readiness. Guy Fawkes was condemned to be hanged, along with others of his fellow-conspirators. So ever since, as November 5th approaches, children make a "guy" out of straw and beg for money to buy fireworks; and on the night of November 5, they let off fireworks and burn the guy on a big bonfire.

April Fools' Day (April 1st) is hardly a festival, but on that day you may find that someone has tied your shoe-laces together, or given you a false message from your employer, or played some practical jokes on you to make you an "April Fool."

A birthday is a purely personal festival. The twenty-first birthday is a great event, since it makes the beginning of full manhood or womanhood, when a person is said to have "reached his majority." The birthday of the British Monarch is a National Day in Britain, for there is no fixed day which is a National Day in Britain. Queen Elizabeth was born on April 21st, 1926. Because the weather in April is usually not good, national celebrations are held on the second Thursday of June every year.

There are many other smaller festivals, like wedding anniversaries, Mother's Day, various saints' days, St George's Day (April 23rd) in England, and St Patrick's Day (March 17th) in Northern Ireland and local customs. The only really important patriotic festival is Remembrance Sunday, which is the Sunday nearest to November 11th. On this Sunday the dead of both world wars are remembered in special church services and civic ceremonies, the chief of which is the laying of wreathes at the Cenotaph, London by members of the royal family in the presence of leading statesmen and politicians (including the Prime Minister and Leader of the Opposition).

Official public holidays are also called "Bank Holidays." The term "Bank Holiday" goes back to the Bank Holidays act of 1871, which owes its name to the fact that banks are closed on the days specified. The public holidays in Great Britain are as follows:

January 1st: New Year's Day

January 2nd: Bank Holiday (Scotland only)

March / April: Good Friday

Easter Monday (not Scotland)

May (first Monday): May Day Bank Holiday

May (last Monday): Spring Bank Holiday

August (last Monday): Summer Bank Holiday (not Scotland)

December 25th: Christmas Day

December 26th: Boxing Day (It was formerly the custom to give "Christmas boxes," or gifts of money, to servants and tradesmen on this day. Today many people still give an annual Christmas gift to regular callers such as dustmen and paperboys.)

The British calendar is full of holidays and festivals which demonstrate the different cultures and histories of the people who make up Britain. Holiday customs have changed as times have changed. Ancient pagan traditions were adapted by the church as Britain became a nation of Christians. Now that the Christian church is not as influential as it was in the past, Christian holidays and customs have changes again so they can be shared by people throughout the country whatever their backgrounds and beliefs. Thus Welsh people can celebrate Burns night, Londoners can watch Dragon Dances at Chinese New Year. Muslims can enjoy chocolate Easter eggs and Christians can go shopping on Boxing Day. Such holidays remind us of how cultures change and influence each other; they also give us an opportunity to share in the rich cultural heritage of the United Kingdom.

## ▼ A Short Story ▼

### The Spring Bank Holiday

The Spring Bank Holiday, also known as the Late May Bank Holiday, is a time for people in the United Kingdom to have a day off work or school. It falls on the last Monday of May but it used to be on the Monday after Pentecost.

## What Do People Do?

For many people the Spring Bank Holiday is a pleasant day off work or school. Some people choose to take a short trip or vacation. Others use the time to walk in the country, catch up with family and friends, visit garden centers or do home maintenance. However, in some parts of the United Kingdom, there are some customs associated with this day.

On Cooper's Hill in Brockworth, Gloucestershire, people race down a steep hill following a large round cheese. The hill is concave and has an incline of 1:1 in some places. The first person to cross the finishing line wins a Double Gloucester cheese weighing about 8 lbs (around 3.5 kg). The custom may have been started by the Romans or ancient Britons and be an ancient fertility rite or a way of guaranteeing the rights of the villagers to graze their livestock on the surrounding land. In some years, there have been a lot of injuries, causing the event to be cancelled a couple of times in recent years. In these years, the cheese was rolled down the hill, but nobody was allowed to chase it.

In Endon in Staffordshire, the villagers dress their well, hold a fayre (village celebration) and crown a girl as the Well Dressing Queen. Local men hold a competition, known as "Tossing the Sheaf," in which they compete to see who can toss a bale of straw the highest. In other places, boats are blessed, Morris dancers put on displays and local festivals are held.

## Background

The Spring Bank Holiday is known as Whitsun or Whit Monday in the United Kingdom. The *Banking and Financial Dealings Act 1971,* moved this bank holiday to the last Monday in May, following a trial period of this arrangement from 1965 to 1970.

In 2002 this bank holiday was moved to June 4 to follow an extra bank holiday on June 3. This gave people a four-day weekend to celebrate the Golden Jubilee of Queen Elizabeth Ⅱ. This marked the 50th year of her accession to the throne of the United Kingdom. The Spring Bank Holiday was also moved to June 4 in 2012, to form a long weekend along with the Queen's Diamond Jubilee Bank Holiday.

## ··· *Exercises* ···

### 【Fill in the Blanks】

1. There are two kinds of horse racing: racing and _____.

2. Traditionally, people gave Christmas gifts or money to their staff or servants on _____, which is the day after Christmas.

3. The FA stands for _____.

4. The Bonfire Night, which is celebrated in November, sometimes is also called _____.

5. Overseas Chinese community in Britain often celebrates Chinese New Year with _____ dances and fireworks.

### 【Multiple Choices】

1. On which day is Halloween celebrated?

   A. October 31st.            B. November 5th.

   C. March 17th.             D. December 25th.

2. Of which people is Robert Burns as a national poet?

   A. The Welsh people.        B. The Irish people.

   C. The Scottish people.     D. The English people.

3. Which celebration particularly happens on the Queen's birthday?

   A. Bonfires.               B. The Orange March.

   C. Trooping the Color.      D. Masqueraded.

4. Which community observes the traditional Ramadan?

   A. Hindu.       B. Sikh.       C. Jewish.       D. Muslim.

5. Easter commemorates _____.

   A. the birth of Jesus Christ

   B. the Crucifixion of Jesus Christ

   C. the coming of spring

   D. the Crucifixion and Resurrection of Jesus Christ

【Discussion】

1. Which festival is the greatest in Britain? What is its significance and at what time is it celebrated?
2. What is the Scottish tradition concerning New Year's Day?
3. How is Christmas usually celebrated in Britain?

# Part II

# The United States

Unit 11

# General Introduction

Deciduous vegetation and grasslands prevail in the east, changing to prairies, north forests, and the Rockies in the west, and deserts in the southwest. In the northeast, the coasts of the Great Lakes and Atlantic seaboard host much of the country's population.

Forty-eight of the states are in the single region between Canada and Mexico; this group is referred to, as the continental United States, and as the Lower 48. Alaska, is at the northwestern end of North America, separated from the Lower 48 by Canada.

The capital city, Washington, District of Columbia, is a federal district located on land donated by the state of Maryland. (Virginia had also donated land, but it was returned in 1849.) The United States also has overseas territories with varying levels of independence and organization: in the Caribbean the territories of Puerto Rico and the U.S. Virgin Islands, and in the Pacific the inhabited territories of Guam, American Samoa, and the Northern Mariana Islands, along with a number of uninhabited island territories.

The United States of America locates in central and northwest North America with coastlines on the Atlantic and Pacific oceans. The country is bordered by Canada on the north, Mexico and Gulf Mexico on the south, the Atlantic Ocean on the west. The total area of the USA is 9,629,091 square km (The area of land is 9,158,960 square km). The length of land is 4,500 km, the width is 2, 700 km and the coastline is 22, 680 km. It includes the noncontiguous states of Alaska and Hawaii and various island territories in the Caribbean Sea and Pacific Ocean.

From 1989 through 1996, the total area of the U.S. was listed as 9,372,610 square km (land + inland water only). The listed total area changed to 9,629,091 square km in 1997 (Great Lakes area and coastal waters added), to 9,631,418 square km in 2004, to 9,631,420 square km in 2006, and to 9,826,630 square km in 2007 (territorial waters added). Currently, the CIA World Factbook gives 9,826,675 square km, the United Nations Statistics Division gives 9,629,091 square km, and the Encyclopedia Britannica gives 9,522,055 square km (Great Lakes area included but not coastal waters). These sources consider only the 50 states and the Federal District, and exclude overseas territories.

By total area (water as well as land), the United States is either slightly larger or smaller than the People's Republic of China, making it the world's third or fourth largest country. China and the United States are smaller than Russia and Canada in total area, but are larger than Brazil. By land area only (exclusive of waters), the United States is the world's third largest country, after Russia and China, with Canada in fourth.

The terrain of American is high in the west and east, while low in the middle area. The terrain is dominated by plains and mountains, and is distributed in the north-south longitudinal column. The mainland can be divided into three physiographic divisions: The eastern part is highlands. The Appalachian Range stretches almost unbroken Alabama to the Canadian border beyond. The western part is high plateaus and mountains. The whole area of this part holds one third of the country's territory on the continent. Then the third part is the Great Plains. It contains a series of lowland, which stretch from the Great Lakes in the north to the Gulf of Mexico in the south.

The eastern United States has a varied topography. A broad, flat coastal plain lines the Atlantic and Gulf shores from the Texas-Mexico border to New York City. The Appalachian Mountains form a line of low mountains separating the eastern seaboard from the Great Lakes and the Mississippi Basin. West of the Appalachians lies the Mississippi River basin and two large eastern tributaries, the Ohio River and the Tennessee River. The Ohio and Tennessee Valleys and the Midwest consist largely of rolling hills and productive farmland, stretching south to the Gulf Coast.

The Rocky Mountains form a large portion of the Western U.S., entering from Canada and stretching nearly to Mexico. The Rocky Mountain region is the highest region of the United States by average elevation. The Rocky Mountains generally contain fairly mild slopes and wider peaks compared to some of the other great mountain ranges, with a few exceptions (such as the Teton Mountains in Wyoming and the Sawatch Range in Colorado). The highest peaks of the Rockies are found in Colorado, the tallest peak being Mount Elbert at 4,400 m. The Rocky Mountains contain some of the most spectacular, and well known scenery in the world.

Between the Appalachians and the Rocky Mountains, lies the vast interior plain of the United States—The Great Plains. The great interior plain consists of two major sub-regions: the fertile Central Plains, extending from the Appalachian highlands to a line drawn approximately 480 km west of the Mississippi, broken by the Ozark Plateau; and the more arid Great Plains, extending from that line to the foothills of the Rocky Mountains. Although they appear flat, the Great Plains rise gradually from about 460 m to more than 1,500 m at their western extremity. The Great Plains come to an abrupt end at the Rocky Mountains. The lowest point in the United States is Death Valley in California, 86 m below sea level. At 6,194 m, Mt. McKinley in Alaska is the highest peak in North America.

The Mississippi River is the chief river of the second largest drainage system on the North American continent, second only to the Hudson Bay drainage system. Flowing entirely in the United States (although its drainage basin reaches into Canada), it rises in northern Minnesota and meanders slowly southwards for 3,730 km to the Mississippi River Delta at the Gulf of Mexico.

The Mississippi River has the world's fourth largest drainage basin ("watershed" or "catchment"). The basin covers more than 3,220,000 square km, including all or parts of 31 U.S. states and two Canadian provinces. The drainage basin empties into the Gulf of Mexico, part of the Atlantic Ocean. The total catchment of the Mississippi River covers nearly 40% of the landmass of the continental United States.

Mississippi Waters, starting from the source of the Missouri, travel almost 6,450 km to the Gulf of Mexico. The eastern reaches of the great interior plain are bounded on the north by the Great Lakes, which are thought to contain about half the world's total supply of fresh water.

Located in the north-central portion of the country, The Great Lakes is the largest lakes in the world. It consists of Lake Superior, the largest freshwater lake in the world; Lake Humor, Lake Michigan, the largest lake that is entirely within one country; Lake Erie and Lake Ontario. Due to their sea-like characteristics (rolling waves, sustained winds, strong currents, great depths, and distant horizons), the five Great Lakes have also long been referred to as inland seas. Lake Superior is the second largest lake in the world by area, and Lake Michigan is the only one located entirely in the United States. The southern half of the Great Lakes is bordered by the Great Lakes Megalopolis.

Due to its large size and wide range of geographic features, the United States contains examples of nearly every global climate. The climate is temperate in most areas, subtropical in the Southern United States, tropical in Hawaii and southern Florida, polar in Alaska, semiarid in the Great Plains west of the 100th meridian, Mediterranean in coastal California and arid in the Great Basin. Its comparatively favorable agricultural climate contributed (in part) to the country's rise as a world power, with infrequent severe drought in the major agricultural regions, a general lack of widespread flooding, and a mainly temperate climate that receives adequate precipitation.

The Great Basin and Columbia Plateau (the Intermontane Plateaus) are arid or semiarid regions that lie in the rain shadow of the Cascades and Sierra Nevada. The Southwest is a hot desert, with temperatures exceeding 37.8 ℃ for several weeks at a time in summer. The Southwest and the Great Basin are also affected by the monsoon from the Gulf of California from July to September, which brings localized but often severe thunderstorms to the region.

Much of California consists of a Mediterranean climate, with sometimes excessive rainfall from October to April and nearly no rain in the rest of the year. In the Pacific Northwest rain falls year-round, but is much heavier during winter and spring. The mountains of the west receive abundant precipitation and very heavy snowfall. The Cascades are one of the snowiest places in the world, with some places averaging over 600 inches (1,524 cm) of snow annually, but the lower elevations closer to the coast receive very little snow.

Florida has a subtropical climate in the northern and central part of the state and a tropical climate in the far southern part of the state. Summers are wet and winters are dry in Florida. Annually much of central and southern Florida is frost-free. The mild winters of Florida allow a massive citrus industry to thrive in the central part of the state, and Florida is second to only Brazil in citrus production in the world.

Another significant (but localized) weather effect is lake-effect snow that falls south and east of the Great Lakes, especially in the hilly portions of the Upper Peninsula of Michigan and on the Tug Hill Plateau in New York. The Wasatch Front and Wasatch Range in Utah can also receive significant lake effect accumulations from the Great Salt Lake. The climate of the United States varies due to differences in latitude, and a range of geographic features, including mountains and deserts. Most regions of the United States are temperate and subtropical.

The characteristics of precipitation across the United States differ significantly across the United States and its possessions. Late summer and fall extratropical cyclones bring a majority of the precipitation which falls across western, southern, and southeast Alaska annually. During the fall, winter, and spring, Pacific storm systems bring most of Hawaii and the western United States much of their precipitation.

In the central and upper eastern United States, precipitation is evenly distributed throughout the year, although summer rainfall increases as one moves southeastward, until a sharp wet summer and dry winter prevail in Florida. Lake-effect snows add to precipitation potential downwind of the Great Lakes, as well as Great Salt Lake and the Finger Lakes during the cold season. The average snow to liquid ratio across the contiguous United States is 13:1, meaning 330 mm of snow melts down to 25 mm of water.

The United States is affected by a variety of natural disasters yearly. Although drought is rare, it has occasionally caused major disruption, such as during the Dust Bowl (1931-1942). Farmland failed throughout the Plains, entire regions were virtually depopulated, and dust storms ruined the land.

The Great Plains and Midwest, due to the contrasting air masses, sees frequent severe thunderstorms and tornado outbreaks during spring and summer with around 1,000 tornadoes occurring each year.

Hurricane season runs from June 1st to November 30th, with a peak from mid-August through early October. Some of the more devastating hurricanes have included the Galveston Hurricane of 1900, Hurricane Andrew in 1992, and Hurricane Katrina in 2005. The remnants of tropical cyclones from the Eastern Pacific also occasionally impact the western United States, bringing moderate to heavy rainfall.

Occasional severe flooding is experienced. There was the Great Mississippi Flood of 1927, the Great Flood of 1993, and widespread flooding and mudslides caused by the 1982-1983 El Niño event in the western United States. Localized flooding can, however, occur anywhere, and mudslides from heavy rain can cause problems in any mountainous area, particularly the Southwest. Large stretches of desert shrub in the west can fuel the spread of wildfires.

Other natural disasters include: tsunamis around Pacific Basin, mudslides in California, and forest fires in the western half of the contiguous U.S. Although drought is relatively rare, it has occasionally caused major economic and social disruption, such as during the Dust Bowl (1931-1942), which resulted in widespread crop failures and dust storms, beginning in the southern Great Plains and reaching to the Atlantic Ocean.

The United States abounds with natural resources. Ore resource like coal, oil, natural gas, iron ore, potash, phosphate and sulphur are among the highest in the world. Strategic mineral resources titanium, manganese, cobalt and chromium are mainly imported. Proven coal reserves are 35,966 million tons. Proven crude oil reserves are 27 billion barrels. The natural gas reserves were 56,03.4 billion cubic meters. The forest area is about 4.4 billion mu, with a coverage rate of 33%.

Take oil for example. U.S. proven oil reserves were 26.5 billion barrels as of 2011. The 2011 data represent a 39% increase in proved reserves since 2008. Proven oil reserves in the United States were 36.4 billion barrels of crude oil as of the end of 2014, excluding the Strategic Petroleum Reserve. The 2014 reserves represent the largest U.S. proven reserves since 1972, and a 90% increase in proved reserves since 2008. The Energy Information Administration estimates U.S. undiscovered, technically recoverable oil resources, to be an additional 198 billion barrels. The United States Geological Survey (USGS) estimates undiscovered technically recoverable crude oil onshore in United States to be 48.5 billion barrels.

The U.S. ecology is megadiverse: about 17,000 species of vascular plants occur in the contiguous United States and Alaska, and over 1,800 species of flowering plants are found in Hawaii, few of which occur on the mainland. The United States is home to 428 mammal species, 784 bird species, 311 reptile species, and 295 amphibian species. About 91,000 insect species have been described. The bald eagle is both the national bird and national animal of the United States, and is an enduring symbol of the country itself.

The native flora of the United States includes about 17,000 species of vascular plants, plus tens of thousands of additional species of other plants and plant-like organisms such as algae, lichens and other fungi, and mosses. About 3,800 additional non-native species of vascular plants are recorded as established outside of cultivation in the U.S., as well as a much smaller number of non-native non-vascular plants and plant relatives. The United States possesses one of the most diverse temperate floras in the world, comparable only to that of China.

The National Park System of the United States is the collection of physical properties owned or administered by the National Park Service. This includes all areas designated national parks and most national monuments, as well as several other types of protected areas of the United States.

There are 58 national parks and hundreds of other federally managed parks, forests, and wilderness areas. Altogether, the government owns about 28% of the country's land area. Most of this is protected, though some is leased for oil and gas drilling, mining, logging, or cattle ranching.

## *A Short Story*

### The Star-Spangled Banner

"The Star-Spangled Banner" is the national anthem of the United States of America. The lyrics come from "Defence of Fort M'Henry", a poem written on September 14, 1814, by the 35-year-old lawyer and amateur poet Francis Scott Key after witnessing the bombardment of Fort McHenry by British ships of the Royal Navy in Baltimore Harbor during the Battle of Baltimore in the War of 1812. Key was inspired by the large American flag, the Star-Spangled Banner, flying triumphantly above the fort during the American victory.

The poem was set to the tune of a popular British song written by John Stafford Smith for the Anacreontic Society, a men's social club in London. "To Anacreon in Heaven" (or "The Anacreontic Song"), with various lyrics, was already popular in the United States. Set to Key's poem and renamed "The Star-Spangled Banner," it soon became a well-known American patriotic song. With a range of one octave and one fifth (a semitone more than an octave and a half), it is known for being difficult to sing. Although the poem has four stanzas, only the first is commonly sung today.

"The Star-Spangled Banner" was recognized for official use by the United States Navy in 1889, and by U.S. President Woodrow Wilson in 1916, and was made the national anthem by a congressional resolution on March 3, 1931, which was signed by President Herbert Hoover.

Before 1931, other songs served as the hymns of American officialdom. "Hail, Columbia" served this purpose at official functions for most of the 19th century. "My Country, 'Tis of Thee," whose melody is identical to "God Save the Queen," the British national anthem, also served as a de facto anthem. Following the War of 1812 and subsequent American wars, other songs emerged to compete for popularity at public events, among them "The Star-Spangled Banner," as well as "America the Beautiful."

## ▪▪▪ *Exercises* ▪▪▪

【Fill in the Blanks】

1. Of all the states _____ is the largest in area and _____ Island the smallest.

2. The New World of America was formed as a result of two long-continuing immigration movements, the first one from _____ and the second from _____ and _____.

3. The crop _____ that was transplanted from the West Indian saved Virginia.

4. The Hawaii Islands were formed by _____ that erupted on the _____ floor.

5. Columbus discovered the New World in the year of _____.

【Multiple Choices】

1. The United States is the _____ largest country in size in the world.

   A. the first        B. the second        C. the third        D. the fourth

2. One of the most important lakes in the United States is _____, which is the largest fresh water lake in the world.

   A. Lake Superior    B. Lake Michigan    C. Lake Huron    D. Lake Ontario

3. The Missouri rises in southwest _____ among the Rocky Mountains.

   A. Illinois        B. Montana        C. Ohio        D. Cairo

4. _____ is sometimes called the birthplace of America.

   A. New Jersey       B. New England       C. Indiana       D. Wisconsin

5. The following were the main Reformation leaders except _____.

   A. Martin Luther

   B. Martin Luther King

   C. John Calvin

   D. the English King Henry Ⅷ

【Discussion】

1. Describe the features of mountains in the U.S.
2. Briefly introduce the main disasters in the U.S.
3. What is the main feature of American resources?

# Unit 12

【Discussion】

1. Describe the features of mountains in the U.S.

2. Briefly introduce the main disasters in the U.S.

3. What is the main feature of American resources?

## Courts

### State Courts

For the most part, law in the United States can be conveniently classified, as decisional law and legislation. Custom, a third possibility, is relatively insignificant as a source of law. It may be used, for example, in interpreting a contract or in determining whether a prescribed standard of conduct has been met. The judicial system is the most appropriate starting point for an inquiry into the sources of law for, so the judiciary has been the traditional source of law in America as in other common law countries. One of the results of the particular form of federalism is a judicial structure in which a nationwide system of federal courts functions alongside the courts of the fifty states.

The great bulk of all litigation comes before the state courts. Each state by constitution and statute has established its own system, and the lack of uniformity makes it impossible to give a detailed description to fit all states. In the late eighteenth century, when the first court systems were established, travel was difficult and communication was slow. The response was to create a number of courts of general jurisdiction to bring justice close to the people, who soon regarded the state court in their locality as their own particular possession. This policy of multiplication of courts and decentralization of the court system has persisted until modem times. In recent years, however, considerable progress has been made in the simplification of state court systems partly through the efforts of the American Judicature Society and the judicial councils.

In each state there are trial courts of general jurisdiction which are called by such names as district, superior, or circuit courts or courts of common pleas. A single judge presides, and is generally competent to hear all cases, civil and criminal, which are not restricted to special courts or divisions. Such special courts or divisions may include criminal courts, family or domestic relations courts, juvenile or children's courts, and probate or surrogates' courts for decedents' estates. In addition, there are courts of inferior jurisdiction which handle petty matters. These were traditionally the justice of the peace courts, but they have often been replaced by county, municipal, small claims, police, and traffic courts. Neither at the state nor the federal level are there special administrative or commercial courts.

At the top of the state judicial system is the highest appellate court of that state. In most states it is called simply the Supreme Court; in some it is known by another name, such as the court of appeals in New York and in several other states. The number of judges ranges from three to nine, with seven the most common number, including a chief justice and associate justices. The growing number of appeals has produced two devices to handle the increased business of the state appellate courts. In some states the highest court sits in separate divisions, or panels, each with general jurisdiction and with provision for the resolution of inconsistencies among the decisions of these divisions. In others there are intermediate appellate courts, between the courts of general jurisdiction and the highest court. In the largest number of states, however, there is neither a separate division of the highest court nor an intermediate appellate court.

## Federal Courts

The decision of the framers of the Constitution to leave to Congress the creation of lower federal courts, has given flexibility and the opportunity for experiment to the federal judicial system. This system has three principal levels: the district courts, the courts of appeals, and the Supreme Court. There are also such special courts of limited jurisdiction as the Court of Claims, the Customs Court, the Court of Customs and Patent Appeals, and the Court of Military Appeals. Although there is no special system of administrative courts, there are, many federal administrative tribunals.

The district courts are the trial courts of general jurisdiction for both civil and criminal cases and may sit as bankruptcy or admiralty courts as well. They also review the decisions of some federal administrative agencies. There are eighty-six district courts located throughout the fifty states. Some states contain only one judicial district, while others are divided into as many as four judicial districts. The territorial jurisdiction of a district court extends, only within the state where it is located. Although a judicial district may have a number of judges, a single judge general presides over both jury and non-jury cases. In some special cases file court must consist of three judges, one of whom must be a member of a higher federal court.

Appeals from a district court are generally heard in the court of appeals for the circuit in which the district is located. There are eleven such circuits, ten comprising geographical divisions of the states and including a number of districts and an eleventh for the District of Columbia. These are the intermediary appellate courts in the federal system, but they are, in fact, the courts of last resort for most federal cases. In addition to hearing appeals from the district courts, they also review decisions of certain federal administrative agencies such as the National Labor Relations Board. The number of judges in each circuit varies, but the judges ordinarily hear appeals in panels of three.

Appellate review of the decisions of the courts of appeals is in the hands of the Supreme Court, one chief justice and eight associate justices, who sit as a body and not in panels. Their number is fixed by Congress. It is the only federal court created by the Constitution; all others are creatures of congressional enactment under a grant of power in the Constitution. As will be explained shortly, it is not only the highest appellate court of the federal system, but also has a limited power of review over the state courts. However, the proportion of cases in which either sort of review is in fact allowed is very small.

## ▶ A Short Story ◀

### The Court of Claims

The Court of Claims was a federal court that heard claims against the

United States government. It was established in 1855, renamed in 1948 to the United States Court of Claims, and abolished in 1982. Then, its jurisdiction was assumed by the newly created United States Court of Appeals for the Federal Circuit and United States Claims Court, which was later renamed the Court of Federal Claims.

Before the Court of Claims was established, monetary claims against the federal government were normally submitted through petitions to Congress. By the time of the Court's creation, the workload had become unwieldy so Congress gave the Court jurisdiction to hear all monetary claims based upon a law, a regulation, or a federal government contract. The Court was required to report its findings to Congress and to prepare bills for payments to claimants whose petitions were approved by the Court. Since only Congress was constitutionally empowered to make appropriations, Congress still had to approve the bills and reports, but it usually did so pro forma.

The Court originally had three judges, who were given lifetime appointments. The judges were authorized to appoint commissioners to take depositions and issue subpoenas. The federal government was represented in the Court by a solicitor appointed by the President.

## ▪▪▪ Exercises ▪▪▪

【Fill in the Blanks】

1. The first period of the party system arose in the last years of the _____ century.

2. The Congress has many functions, but the most central is _____.

3. The President of the United States is head of the _____ branch.

4. Membership in the House of Representatives is based on _____.

5. The Supreme Court has _____ and eight associate justices.


【Multiple Choices】

1. The second highest level of the federal judiciary is made up of _____.

   A. the Supreme Court                    B. the House of Representatives

C. the Courts of Appeals        D. the White House

2. Abraham Lincoln, as candidate of the _____ Party, was elected President in 1860.

   A. Democratic    B. Republican    C. Labor    D. Conservative

3. The Constitution grants all legislative power of the federal government to a _____ composed of two chambers.

   A. Congress                 B. Senate

   C. Supreme Court        D. Department of State

4. The American federal government has _____ layers of rule.

   A. one       B. two       C. three       D. four

5. _____ is the basic instrument of American government and the supreme law of the land.

   A. *Declaration of Independence*    B. *The Bill of Rights*

   C. *The Constitution of the U.S.*    D. *The Bible*

【Discussion】

1. Describe the differences of the two courts in the U.S.

2. What are the potential loopholes of the current system of courts?

# Religion

Freedom of religion in America precludes asking anyone about personal religious beliefs, whether in job interviews or even in the decennial federal census. The federal government has never collected data on religious adherence. Determining numbers of members of denominations or churches is, therefore, dependent on surveys by various organizations or the denominations themselves. The fact that different religious groups count different things (baptized vs. active members, for example) further confounds efforts to understand American religion through numbers. Nevertheless, a look at the big picture is instructive.

Most Americans believe in God; only around 2 or 3 percent of the population are agnostics or atheists. The United States is about 80 percent Christian; data from independent surveys vary from over 76 to 82 percent. Around 13 percent of Americans are nonreligious or secular, and about 2 percent are Jewish. No other religions—Greek Orthodox, Russian Orthodox, Islam, Hinduism, Buddhism, Druidism, Sikhism, Scientology, Deism, Taoist, New Age, or Native American—are believed to approach 1 percent of the population.

The 10 largest religious bodies in the United States are the Roman Catholic Church with 67.8 million; the Southern Baptist Convention, with 16.2 million; the United Methodist Church, with 8.2 million; the Church of Jesus Christ of Latter-day Saints, with 6 million; the Church of God in Christ (Black Pentecostal), with 5.5 million; the National Baptist Convention, USA, with 5 million; the Evangelical Lutheran Church of America, with 4.9 million; the National Baptist Convention of America, with 3.5 million; the Presbyterian

Church (USA), with 3.2 million; and the Assemblies of God (USA), with 2.8 million. The largest 25 denominations in the United States account for over 148 million people.

Evangelical Protestants (Baptists, Reformed and Confessional churches, nondenominational Christians, Pentecostals, Churches of Christ, etc.) equal the Roman Catholic population at about 25 percent. Mainline White Protestant churches (Methodists, Lutherans, Presbyterians, Episcopalians, and Congregationalists) are about 22 percent of the population. African American Protestants make up about 8 percent of the population.

It is a sad fact of American life that white and African American people could not worship together equally as God's children. Racism permeated every niche of society. On the other hand, owing to the enterprise of early African American religious leaders, African American churches were founded that would become the bedrock religious and social foundation of African American society. The African American churches were legally untouchable and totally independent thanks to the First Amendment. They were also in fact the only African American institutions in America—places where African American culture could flourish, places where African Americans could find pride and independence, places where African Americans were in charge. The Reverend Martin Luther King coordinated the civil rights movement through African American churches. Today, African American churches continue their proud traditions and work for the economic empowerment of the African American population.

American Protestant churches have been divided by race as well as by biblical interpretation. Evangelicals, who believe in a literal, strict interpretation of the *Bible*, have generally shunned social action in favor of personal salvation. Evangelicalism has therefore been inherently individualistic in seeking in its adherents the personal transformation. As a result, evangelicals generally remained aloof from the social and political landscape of the country, until their political power was unleashed by conservative activists. The mainline Protestant churches are not as likely to insist on literal biblical interpretation and have emphasized the importance of social action as a means toward salvation. It was these churches, therefore, that actively developed charitable enterprises to serve the poor and disenfranchised and became active in political and social issues and movements.

Fundamentalism, as much a creed as a state of mind, has been a constant force against modernism in American life, even though it was thought many times to have vanished. The name derives from the publication between 1910 and 1915 of *The Fundamentals: A Testimony to the Truth* in 12 volumes. Fundamentalists are evangelicals who believe in the religious, scientific, and historical truth of the *Bible*: Jesus Christ's divinity, virgin birth, atonement for mankind's sins by death on the cross, resurrection from the dead, and the return of Jesus Christ on Judgment Day to judge the living and the dead. Fundamentalists also believe in Bible prophecy.

Armed with biblical truth, fundamentalists have been persistent, if not militant, guerilla warriors in the fight to make their vision of a Christian America come true. This vision harkens back to an America that existed only ideally, but before expositors questioned the literal meaning of the *Bible*, before women questioned their traditional roles, before gay rights was a topic of discussion, before evolution became an accepted theory, and before abortion was legalized. Fundamentalists believe they are preserving traditional American values that so-called liberal churches, liberal politicians, and modern American culture have helped to erode. They have enjoyed being outsiders who can pick and choose their battles emboldened by independence. A simple, understandable America prepared for Judgment Day is especially appealing in times of social change and uncertainty. Waves of revivalism swept the country during the Roaring Twenties, during World War II, and in the Vietnam War era.

The American religious landscape is changing rapidly at the turn of the twenty-first century. The Roman Catholic Church continues to grow in absolute numbers with the influx of traditional Catholics from Mexico, even as it closes churches in the inner cities of the Northeast and Midwest. The number of Roman Catholics would be growing even more, but Evangelical Protestantism has made inroads into that population. Over 30 percent of

Mexicans coming into the United States are believed to be evangelicals, even though they may maintain traditional Roman Catholic practices and, indeed, may return to Catholicism. The membership in mainline Protestant churches appears to be dwindling in comparison to the burst in evangelical numbers. Americans also seem to be attracted to nondenominational, Bible-based megachurches with congregations of more than 20,000.

There can be no doubt that America is in the midst of another wave of religious awakening. It is evangelical, if not sometimes Pentecostal. It is black and white and multicolored. It is largely Protestant. Americans want traditional American values, not a tax code-sized volume of church canons. It is *New Testament*; it is simple; it is salvation from uncertainty, social disconnection, and the vagaries of terrorism.

The most popular religion in the U.S. is Christianity, comprising the majority of the population (70.6% of adults in 2014). According to the Association of Statisticians of American Religious Bodies newsletter published March 2017, based on data from 2010, Christians were the largest religious population in all 3,143 counties in the country. Roughly 46.5% of Americans are Protestants, 20.8% are Catholics, 1.6% are Mormons.

According to a 2012 review by the National Council of Churches, the five largest denominations are:

The Catholic Church, 68,202,492 members;

The Southern Baptist Convention, 16,136,044 members;

The United Methodist Church, 7,679,850 members;

The Church of Jesus Christ of Latter-day Saints, 6,157,238 members;

The Church of God in Christ, 5,499,875 members.

The Southern Baptist Convention, with over 16 million adherents, is the largest of more than 200 distinctly named Protestant denominations. In 2007, members of evangelical churches comprised 26% of the American population, while another 18% belonged to mainline Protestant churches, and 7% belonged to historically black churches.

Historians agree that members of mainline Protestant denominations have played leadership roles in many aspects of American life, including politics, business, science, the arts, and education. They founded most of the country's leading institutes of higher education. According to Harriet Zuckerman, 72% of American Nobel Prize Laureates between 1901 and 1972 have identified from Protestant background.

Some of the first colleges and universities in America, including Harvard, Yale, Princeton, Columbia, Dartmouth, Williams, Bowdoin, Middlebury, and Amherst, all were founded by mainline Protestant denominations. By the 1920s most had weakened or dropped their formal connection with a denomination. James Hunter argues that: The private schools and colleges established by the mainline Protestant denominations, as a rule, still want to be known as places that foster values, but few will go so far as to identify those values as Christian... . Overall, the distinctiveness of mainline Protestant identity has largely dissolved since the 1960s.

Beginning around 1600 European settlers introduced Anglican and Puritans religion, as well as Baptist, Presbyterian, Lutheran, Quaker, and Moravian denominations.

Beginning in the 16th century, the Spanish (and later the French and English) introduced Catholicism. From the 19th century to the present, Catholics came to the U.S. in large numbers due to immigration of Italians, Hispanics, Portuguese, French, Polish, Irish, Highland Scots, Dutch, Flemish, Hungarians, Germans, Lebanese (Maronite), and other ethnic groups.

Eastern Orthodoxy was brought to America by Greek, Ukrainian, Armenian, and other immigrant groups.

The largest religion, Christianity, has proportionately diminished since 1990. While the absolute number of Christians rose from 1990 to 2008, the percentage of Christians dropped from 86% to 76%. A nationwide telephone interview of 1,002 adults conducted by The Barna Group found that 70% of American adults believe that God is "the all-powerful, all-knowing creator of the universe who still rules it today," and that 9% of all American adults and 0.5% young adults hold to what the survey defined as a "biblical worldview."

Episcopalian, Presbyterian, Eastern Orthodox and United Church of Christ members have the highest number of graduate and post-graduate degrees per capita of all Christian denominations in the United States, as well as the most high-income earners.

After Christianity, Judaism is the next largest religious affiliation in the U.S., though this identification is not necessarily indicative of religious beliefs or practices. There are between 5.3 and 6.6 million Jews. A significant number of people identify themselves as American Jews on ethnic and cultural grounds, rather than religious ones. For example, 19% of self-identified American Jews do not believe God exists. The 2001 ARIS study projected from its sample that there are about 5.3 million adults in the American Jewish population: 2.83 million adults (1.4% of the U.S. adult population) are estimated to be adherents of Judaism; 1.08 million are estimated to be adherents of no religion; and 1.36 million are estimated to be adherents of a religion other than Judaism. ARIS 2008 estimated about 2.68 million adults (1.2%) in the country identify Judaism as their faith.

Jews have been present in what is now the U.S. since the 17th century, and specifically allowed since the British colonial *Plantation Act 1740*. Although small Western European communities initially developed and grew, large-scale immigration did not take place until the late 19th century, largely as a result of persecutions in parts of Eastern Europe. The Jewish community in the United States is composed predominantly of Ashkenazi Jews whose ancestors emigrated from Central and Eastern Europe. There are, however, small numbers of older (and some recently arrived) communities of Sephardi Jews with roots tracing back to 15th century Iberia (Spain, Portugal, and North Africa). There are also Mizrahi Jews (from the Middle East, Caucasia and Central Asia), as well as much smaller numbers of Ethiopian Jews, Indian Jews, Kaifeng Jews and others from various smaller Jewish ethnic divisions. Approximately 25% of the Jewish American population lives in New York City.

Islam is the third largest faith in the United States, after Christianity and Judaism, representing 0.9% of the population. According to the Association of Statisticians of American Religious Bodies newsletter published in March, 2017, based on data from 2010, Muslims were the largest minority religion in

392 counties out of the 3143 counties in the country. Islam in America effectively began with the arrival of African slaves. It is estimated that about 10% of African slaves transported to the United States were Muslim. Most, however, became Christians, and the United States did not have a significant Muslim population until the arrival of immigrants from Arab and East Asian Muslim areas. According to some experts, Islam later gained a higher profile through the Nation of Islam, a religious group that appealed to black Americans after the 1940s; its prominent converts included Malcolm X and Muhammad Ali. The first Muslim elected in Congress was Keith Ellison in 2006, followed by André Carson in 2008.

Research indicates that Muslims in the United States are generally more assimilated and prosperous than their counterparts in Europe. Like other subcultural and religious communities, the Islamic community has generated its own political organizations and charity organizations.

▶ *A Short Story* ▶

## The Southern Baptist Convention

The Southern Baptist Convention (SBC) is a Christian denomination based in the United States. With more than 15 million members as of 2015, it is the world's largest Baptist denomination, the largest Protestant denomination in the United States, and the second-largest Christian denomination in the United States after the Catholic Church.

The word Southern in Southern Baptist Convention stems from it having been organized in 1845 at Augusta, Georgia, by Baptists in the Southern United States who split with northern Baptists over the issue of slavery, specifically whether Southern slave owners could serve as missionaries. After the American Civil War, another split occurred when most freedmen set up independent black congregations, regional associations, and state and national conventions, such as the National Baptist Convention, which became the second-largest Baptist convention by the end of the 19th century. Others joined new African-American denominations, chiefly the African Methodist

Episcopal Church, which was established in Philadelphia, Pennsylvania in the early 19th century, as the first independent black denomination in the United States.

Since the 1940s, the Southern Baptist Convention has shifted from some of its regional and historical identification. Especially since the late twentieth century, the SBC has sought new members among minority groups and become much more diverse. In addition, while still heavily concentrated in the Southern United States, the Southern Baptist Convention has member churches across the United States and 41 affiliated state conventions.

At its annual convention in 2012, the Southern Baptist Convention elected as President Fred Luter Jr., the first African American to hold the position. He was re-elected president for a second (and final) term at the 2013 meeting. The current president in 2016 is Steve Gaines.

Southern Baptist churches are evangelical in doctrine and practice. As they emphasize the significance of the individual conversion experience, which is affirmed by the person having complete immersion in water for a believer's baptism, they reject the practice of infant baptism. Other specific beliefs based on biblical interpretation can vary somewhat due to their congregational polity, which allows autonomy to each individual local church.

## ▀▀ Exercises ▀▀

【Fill in the Blanks】

1. "WASP" stands for _____.
2. Prayer and *Bible* reading in public schools in the U.S. are _____.
3. The Three Faiths in the U.S. refer to Protestant, _____ and _____.
4. Freedom of religious belief or non-belief is provided in the _____ in the U.S. Constitution.
5. The first Catholic president in the U.S. was _____.

【Multiple Choices】

1. Which of the following was not a Protestant denomination?

   A. The Baptists.                    B. The Catholics.

   C. The Methodists.                  D. The Presbyterians.

2. The fist immigrants in American history came from England and _____.

   A. France       B. Germany       C. Spain       D. the Netherlands

3. Which of the following is true?

   A. Many Catholics are not opposed to abortion.

   B. Many evangelical Protestants do not object to abortion.

   C. Orthodox Jews are for abortion.

   D. Liberal Protestants and Jews join non-believers in maintaining that abortion is a basic right for women.

4. In general, the Cuban-Americans have done the best _____.

   A. politically    B. scientifically    C. economically   D. academically

5. Which of the following is not regarded as one of the three basic religious beliefs?

   A. Protestant.    B. Catholic.       C. Islamic.       D. Judaism.

【Discussion】

1. Describe the basic features of American religion system.

2. What are the main sects of American Christianity?

3. What are the major differences between European and American Christianity?

## Unit 14

# Marriage

The institution of marriage in the United States is constantly being redefined. When British settlers first began to arrive in the 17th century, a wife's status and legal position was closer to property than partnership. Divorce was nearly impossible. However, as the American Revolution began to bring more republican values, even marriage was changed. The conception of marriage began to shift toward ideals of love and partnership. Those ideals were not translated into legal equality until quite recently, but modern conceptions of marriage include relative egalitarianism, in legal, if not always practical, terms.

What exactly is marriage? There are four components, some or all of which may be present: a civil bond, a personal bond, community recognition, and religious recognition. The civil bond represents recognition by the state, such as in the issuance of a marriage license, and the religious recognition of the bond is the affirmation of that bond within the couple's house of worship. The personal bond is the private agreement between two people to share their lives, and the community recognition is the public declaration of that agreement. Couples who elope are no less married than couples who wed in front of 200 of their friends and family members; couples who are legally prohibited from obtaining a civil marriage can commit to each other privately and feel just as married. For instance, before the Civil War, slaves were prohibited from marrying. They nonetheless developed ceremonies of their own within their community that celebrated the personal commitments of devoted couples. To be considered wed, the couple merely needed to jump over a broomstick in the presence of witnesses, In addition, after the Civil War, many states had anti-miscegenation laws, which prohibited African Americans and whites from marrying. The Supreme Court decision in Loving v. Virginia overturned those laws in 1976, despite widespread popular disapproval for interracial marriage. Today, few would bat an eye at an interracial relationship.

The patterns for American marriages have been changing. More and more, young people of both genders are leaving their parents' houses after finishing school (either high school or college) and establishing single homes on their own before deciding to wed. This can be shown by rising age at first marriage. In 1980, the average ages at first marriage were just over 23 years for men and just under 21 years for women; in 2005, that had become 27 and nearly 26 years, respectively. Most Americans do marry eventually, though. By the age of 35, 72 percent of Americans have been married, and by the age of 65, that number rises to 96 percent, except for African American men and women, only 90 percent of whom have ever been married by age 65, and for Asian American women, 99 percent of whom have been married at least once by age 65.

Couples do not necessarily stay married, however. In recent years, there have been approximately 7.5–8 new marriages for every 1,000 Americans, and 3.7 divorces per 1,000 each year. At first glance, that seems to point to a 50 percent divorce rate since the legalization of no-fault divorces around 1960. This conventional wisdom that half of all marriages end in divorce, which is a statistic frequently cited by social conservatives to monger fear for the disappearance of the so-called traditional family arrangement. However, this number is a bit misleading, as any statistician could explain. Very few of those 3.7 divorces are from the marriages formed that year; couples divorce anywhere from 60 days into a marriage to 60 years into it. However, many failed marriages tend to end within the first decade, and most (80%) marriages that fail do so within 20 years.

Additionally, this number of 3.7 divorces per 1,000 people in 2004 shows a decline in gross numbers of divorces per year over the last 25 years: in 1980, there were approximately 5.3 divorces per 1,000 people. The actual longitudinal divorce rate is that approximately 31-35 percent of all marriages will end in divorce, down from the 41 percent of 25 years ago. That statistic shows a growing split by educational attainment as well: college graduates are about half as likely to end up divorced than non-college grads. Perhaps it is the later age at first marriage that contributes to the growing stability of the relationships. Perhaps the greater economic stability of college graduates contributes to stability at home as well. Whatever the reason, American marriages are becoming more stable, not less.

Despite the fact that most people marry at some point in their lives, there are other types of relationships and living arrangements, in addition to legal marriages. In actuality, married couples are in the minority these days. According to 2005 census data, out of 111.1 million households, only 49.7 percent of them were composed of married couples—with or without children. There are a number of factors that contribute to this decline. Because of the rising age at first marriage, many young men and women live alone, after finishing their education but before they get married, accounting for over one-fourth of the remaining households. Additionally, couples increasingly feel free to cohabit without stigma, and that number is rising. These unmarried couples made up 5 percent of the households. There are also households headed only by women or by men as a result of divorce. A fourth factor, the gap in life expectancy between men and women means that women may live for several years as widows.

There are other unmarried couples, who might prefer to get married. But just as African slaves could not wed before the Civil War, they are legally barred from obtaining a civil marriage. Currently, the rights and privileges of marriage are restricted only to heterosexual couples. Indeed, it has only been in the last few decades that other types of couples have been recognized as existing at all. Until as recently as 2003, homosexuality has actually been against the law. Many states had laws in place that prohibited certain sexual acts that could be used to prosecute the behavior of consenting adults within the privacy of their own homes. Though heterosexual privacy had been protected since 1972, it was not until June 2003 that the Supreme Court struck down the sodomy laws of Texas, and all others like it, as unconstitutional in Lawrence v. Texas.

## A Short Story

### The Federal Marriage Amendment

The Federal Marriage Amendment (FMA) (also referred to by proponents as the Marriage Protection Amendment) is a proposed amendment to the United States Constitution which would define marriage in the United States as a union of one man and one woman. The FMA would also prevent judicial extension of marriage rights to same-sex or other unmarried heterosexual couples. An amendment to the U.S. Constitution requires the support of two thirds of each house of Congress and ratification by three fourths of the states. The last Congressional vote on the proposed Amendment occurred in the United States House of Representatives on July 18th, 2006, when the Amendment failed 236 to 187, falling short of the 290 votes required for passage in that body. The Senate has only voted on cloture motions with regard to the proposed Amendment, the last of which was on June 7th, 2006, when the motion failed 49 to 48, falling short of the 60 votes required to allow the Senate to proceed to consideration of the Amendment and the 67 votes required to send the amendment to the states.

## Exercises

【Fill in the Blanks】

1. The conception of marriage began to shift toward ideals of ________ and ________.
2. They nonetheless developed ________ of their own within their community that celebrated the personal commitments of devoted couples.
3. There are also ________ headed only by women or by men as a result of ________.
4. Some stated are ________ over homosexual marriage and civil unions.

【Multiple Choices】

1. In addition, after _____, many stated had ant miscegenation laws, which prohibited African American and whites from marrying.

   A. the WW I
   B. the WW II
   C. the Civil War
   D. the Independent War

2. The Supreme Court decision in Loving v. Virginia overturned those laws in _____.

   A. 1976　　　　B. 1977　　　　C. 1978　　　　D. 1979

3. President _____ put forward a Federal Marriage Amendment during 2004 campaign.

   A. George W. Bush
   B. John Adams
   C. Abraham Lincoln
   D. Bill Clinton

4. _____ Americans incorporate it into modern ceremonies as a reminder of their ethnic heritage.

   A. Asia　　　B. Hispanic　　　C. African　　　D. Traditional

【Discussion】

1. How do Americans define marriage?
2. What is the main attitude of Americans toward divorce?

# Unit 15

## Holidays and Festivals

Holidays in American culture encompass a wide range of events. The closest approach to a list of national holidays is the 10 federal holidays, which represent vacation days given to employees of the federal government and which are often also given as paid holidays by state and private employers: New Year's Day, the birthday of Martin Luther King Jr., Washington's Birthday, Memorial Day, Independence Day, Labor Day, Columbus Day, Veterans Day, Thanksgiving, and Christmas.This federal holiday list scarcely defines what Americans see as events worth celebrating since it omits three of the holidays that Americans celebrate most enthusiastically: Valentine's Day, Mother's Day, and Halloween.

Broadening the definition to include official observances makes almost every day a holiday. There are enough federal observances to average one per week, year-round. Add state observances, and it is possible to pack a dozen holidays into a single day: May 1st is Loyalty Day, Bird Day, Family Day, Law Day, Lei Day, and a national Day of Prayer as well as the first day of month-long commemorations of Asian Americans, families, keeping Massachusetts beautiful, kindness, law enforcement workers, children, composers, senior citizens, the steel industry, and women veterans.

Given that Thanksgiving was a traditional event before it became a federal holiday, perhaps a holiday may be defined as a community festival that gains nationwide popularity. Certainly there are plenty of festivals vying for consumers' leisure and dollars. Popular festival themes include local history, local industry or agriculture, music, ethnic heritage, food, and flowers. A typical festival includes a parade, a craft or art show, food vendors, face painting, musical performances, and possibly a competition to crown a queen or princess from among local young women.

Although it is easy to assume that a festival honoring a community's Swedish heritage or plethora of rattle snakes has roots in the distant past, few festivals predate World War II. One researcher found that in Minnesota, fully 12 percent were part of a Bicentennial-era surge of interest in local history. Festivals do not necessarily grow organically from local tradition, either. When organizers of the Whigham Rattlesnake Roundup were asked why they chose rattle-snakes, they responded that it was their first idea other than a fish fry.

Even when a festival commemorates an historic event, the festival itself may not be historic. In Apache Junction, Arizona, the Lost Dutchman Days festival celebrates the legend of a mysterious vanishing mine supposedly discovered in the 1880s. The festival dates only to 1965, about 15 years after the community was established.

The Lost Dutchman may be a myth, but being fictitious does not stop events from inspiring a festival. Impersonators of characters from Gomer Pyle's fictitious town of Mayberry appear at festivals throughout the rural South, culminating in Mayberry Days in Airy, North Carolina. Mena, Arkansas, celebrates Lum N' Abner Days, based on a radio show that was popular in the 1930s.

Not all community festivals are recent inventions, of course, nor are they all in small towns. In Rochester, New York, the Lilac Festival has been celebrated continuously since 1902 (organizers claim 1892). San Francisco's Chinese New Year was celebrated as early as the 1860s; New Orleans's Mardi Gras is older yet. One researcher argues that the appeal of festivals is how they allow participants to belong to a community with minimal effort or commitment.

Certainly there are plenty of communities vying for membership. In a single weekend in late February, people who list cooking and eating as their favorite leisure activities can choose from seven events. At the top of the food chain is the South Beach Wine and Food Festival. It is a Florida weekend that includes the Food Network Awards and is expected to draw 20,000 gourmets who can afford to spend upward of $1,000 on tickets. While this festival dates only to 2002, the Twin Cities Food and Wine Experience and the Newport Seafood and Wine Festival are somewhat older (13 years and 30 years, respectively) and offer more modest ticket prices.

More accessible, owing to free admission, are the Annual Clam Chowder Cook-off in Santa Cruz, California; the Grant Seafood Festival, which draws 50,000 visitors to Oregon and dates to 1996; the Parke County, Indiana, Maple Syrup Fair; and the Annual Florida Gourd Festival. This last event offers not only classes in gourding, but also free parking for recreational vehicles.

Perhaps the most familiar festivals are the county fair and the state fair. The traditional county fair, with livestock exhibitions, parades, performances, and baking competitions, evolved from agricultural and employment fairs around 1811. It was widely popular before the Civil War. Although only about 20 percent of Americans live in rural areas, county fairs have staying power. Though fewer than 1 percent of the residents of San Mateo County, California, work in farming, fishing, or forestry, the county still holds its fair. Even a completely urbanized county like San Francisco sees periodic efforts to start a county fair.

County fairs are held during the summer, as a precursor to the big event: the state fair. As county fairs became popular, the state fair was a natural way to pit county winners against one another and to showcase the state's agricultural bounty. These larger fairs require a permanent exhibition ground that is also used for other events throughout the year. The State Fair of Texas can gross $2.3 million in a single day.

Most communities put more fervor into their county fair than into celebrating a federal holiday like Washington's birthday. Yet it is unlikely that anyone has ever sent a greeting card to commemorate the San Mateo County Fair. Sending holiday cards is such a thoroughly entrenched American tradition that the term Hallmark holidays is used to describe occasions. Suspected Hallmark holidays range from Valentine's Day and

Mother's Day to more obscure Sweetest Day, Secretary's Day, and Grandparents' Day.

Greeting cards and true holidays from work both became popular at about the same time, the mid-nineteenth century. Until the federal government declared four bank holidays in 1870—Independence Day, Thanksgiving, Christmas, and New Year's Day—there was no connection between a celebration and a day off from work.

While even Christmas was celebrated sporadically for years before becoming a major event, Independence Day has been widely celebrated since 1777. Bands, fireworks, parades, and picnics have been part of the celebration as far back as records go. Today, commemorating independence from Great Britain requires 150 million hotdogs, or approximately one for every two people. No one records how many sheet cakes decorated like a flag with strawberries, blueberries, and whipped cream are served, though the recipe has been a staple of women's magazines since the 1830s. It is also one of the least controversial holidays. Other than a gay rights protest in Philadelphia in 1965, there is little record of the controversies over inclusion that enliven St. Patrick's Day, the Chinese New Year, and Columbus Day. Enjoying outdoor fun raises no public complaints about forgetting the meaning of the day.

For Thanksgiving, the civic meaning slipped away so gradually that little protest surrounds today's custom of serving a large meal amid a long day of watching television. Although the holiday reputedly dates to the Pilgrims' first harvest in 1621, and George Washington established a late November date for a day of thanksgiving in 1789, Thanks-giving was not celebrated consistently until after 1863. In 1941, the date was set as the fourth Thursday in November.

Turkey and pumpkins were considered traditional as early as 1854, but the familiar menu for the largest eating holiday of the year was defined largely by army fare in World War II. The dinner served to soldiers in 1941 started with celery and olives, then included almost all of today's standard fare: roast turkey, sage dressing and giblet gravy, cranberry sauce, candied sweet potatoes and mashed potatoes, hot rolls, a vegetable, salad, and pumpkin pie as well as other desserts. The most crucial missing item was green bean casserole, a recipe invented for Campbell's Soup in 1955. By the early 1990s, cooking mavens were promoting nontraditional menus to spice up the day. Turkey remains the centerpiece, but side dishes are where ethnic communities incorporate their own culinary traditions.

Rest is vital, as the Friday after Thanksgiving marks the kick-off of the holiday shopping season. Although so-called Black Friday is not the heaviest shopping day of the year, the flood of shoppers into stores, provides sufficient mayhem to justify the day's nickname.

The goal of all the shopping is Christmas: the most sentimentalized holiday of the year. While 77 percent of Americans identify as Christians, 95 percent celebrate Christmas. Americans send 1.9 billion holiday cards, cut 20.8 million trees, spend almost $32 billion in department stores alone in December, and mail 1 million packages. Special holiday programming rules the television. The most famous Christmas classic, A Charlie Brown Christmas, mentions the birth of Christ and ends with a loosely Christian message of peace and acceptance, but most of the classic programs from the 1960s are more focused on reminding children that Christmas involves Santa Claus and that Santa brings presents.

The last of the original four holidays is New Year's Day, or the morning after a New Year's Eve party that is supposed to include toasting the strike of midnight with champagne, kissing, and singing "Auld Lang Syne." Once day breaks, about 40 percent of Americans make New Year's resolutions, most often to stop smoking, lose weight, and "be a better person." A WTVU/Marist College poll found that at the end of 2005, 63 percent of those surveyed had kept their resolutions, though men were more likely than women to claim success.

Additional federal holidays were added to the calendar gradually, then generally moved to Mondays with the Uniform Monday Holiday Act of 1968 (actually implemented in 1972). These lengthened weekends were supposed to benefit retailers, but it is doubtful that anyone predicted how thoroughly bargain shopping and mini-vacations would distract attention from the people being honored.

Many of these holidays were somewhat controversial in their origins. For instance, Memorial Day (originally Decoration Day) started in 1866 as a way to honor Union soldiers in the recent Civil War. The South had its own Confederate Memorial Day, most often celebrated on April 26th. It has been noted that African Americans observed federal Memorial Day celebrations, while whites in the South still preferred Confederate Memorial Day. Now settled on the last Monday in May, Memorial Day may be more recognized as an excellent weekend for weddings than as a day of remembrance.

Memorial Day is also often confused with Veterans Day, which honors all who fought, including the living. Like Memorial Day, Veterans Day started with a different name, Armistice Day, and a slightly different purpose: to honor those who fought in World War Ⅰ, then believed to be the war to end all wars. After World War II, the day became a more general celebration for veterans. Of the approximately 24.5 million living veterans in the United States, about one-third fought in World War Ⅱ, while 15 percent fought in Vietnam. Although Veterans Day was among the Monday holidays defined in 1968, it has since returned to its original date of November 11. Appropriate activities for both Memorial Day and Veterans Day include decorating the graves of dead soldiers.

Labor Day, assigned to the first Monday in September, developed in the 1880s as a symbolic day of rest for the workingman. At the time, rest was controversial: even Sundays were commonly workdays. As late as 1910, labor leaders and ministers were lobbying for an eight-hour workday and a six-day workweek. Within the next decade, labor leaders adopted Labor Day as an occasion for speeches promoting unionization. Workers must have achieved some rest; by the 1930s, Labor Day had become a big day for trips to the beach.

While Memorial Day has the Indy 500 race, Labor Day has the Muscular Dystrophy Association telethon, hosted by Jerry Lewis since 1966. Perhaps the temptation to stay parked in front of the television on a beautiful fall day has something to do with the reality that school traditionally starts on the day after Labor Day. The start of the school year assumes some of the character of a holiday in its own right, with the average family spending over $ 500 in 2006.

Also born in the 1880s was the far less controversial holiday honoring the birthday of George Washington. Now popularly believed to be a Presidents' Day that also honors Abraham Lincoln, the holiday remains officially dedicated to Washington alone. However, enthusiasm for celebrating Washington's leadership has waned substantially since 1855, when New Yorkers turned out for a parade with military bands and floats, plus speeches, songs, and fireworks. By the 1980s, the Manhattan parade had been reduced to a parochial school fife-and-drum corps and the Knights of Columbus, and most celebrating was done at Herald Square department stores.

Martin Luther King Day, the newest of federal holidays, demonstrates how a holiday is pulled two ways. Celebrated on the third Monday in January, the day was added to the federal calendar in 1986 to include an African American in the official pantheon of American heroes. The day was not observed in all 50 states until 2000, when New Hampshire renamed its nine-year-old Civil Rights Day. More predictably, the last serious hold out had been South Carolina, which balanced honors for the civil rights leader by adding Confederate Memorial Day to its official state calendar.

With floats and craft booths, Martin Luther King Day may be doing better than Columbus Day, arguably a failure among federal holidays. From its origins in 1869 in San Francisco, Columbus Day was intended to celebrate Italian heritage along with the European discovery of America. The day was added to the official federal calendar in 1937. Since then, observance has lagged. Workplaces stay open; few traditions are associated with the day; the National Retail Federation does not bother to track spending. Hispanics have redefined the day as Día de la Raza, a celebration of Hispanic heritage, while South Dakota celebrates Native American Day.

Meanwhile, an ethnicity that represents less than 1 percent of the population puts on one of the biggest parties on the West Coast: Chinese New

Year in San Francisco. The celebration, dating to the 1860s and held on the lunar New Year in February or early March, rivals New Year events in China and is televised worldwide. The event is so large that Southwest Airlines now sponsors it. And, like the St. Patrick's Day parade in New York, who is in and who is out is a battlefield of identity.

Touching a chord in many lives may be why some festivals grow into holidays. It is hard to oppose honoring mother and father, so there are huge constituencies for celebrating Mother's Day, on the second Sunday in May, and Father's Day, on the third Sunday in June. Both holidays were products of lingering Victorian sentimentality. Anna Jarvis of Grafton, West Virginia, spearheaded Mother's Day in 1908 to honor her late mother. The same year, Grace Golden Clayton of Fairmont, West Virginia, introduced a day to honor fathers killed in a mining accident; two years later, Sonora Smart Dodd of Spokane, Washington, held an event to honor her father's devotion as a single parent. Dodd aggressively promoted the event, which was recognized by Congress in 1956 and became a permanent holiday in 1972.

Mother's Day elicits slightly more spending than Valentine's Day, at an average of $122 per person. According to the National Retail Federation, 85 percent of buyers send greeting cards, 65 percent send flowers, and 32 percent buy gift cards. The enormous greeting card spending is still just 4 percent of annual sales, but Mother's Day is definitely the year's busiest day for phone calls. The tradition most firmly associated with the day is wearing a carnation: red for a living mother and white for a deceased one. However, this practice is an evolution from the original practice of wearing or displaying white carnations to honor all mothers, living or dead.

Father's Day packs nowhere near the emotional wallop of Mother's Day. Only about 100 million cards are sent for Father's Day, versus 150 million for Mother's Day. Hallmark and American Greetings agree that funny cards outsell sentimental ones. While the National Retail Federation mourns that spending is about 20 percent lower than for Mother's Day, the National Restaurant Federation notes that Father's Day is the fourth biggest day of the year for dining out. (The others, in reverse order, are Valentine's Day,

New Year's Eve, and Mother's Day.)

A third holiday devoted to sentiment, St. Valentine's Day on February 14, has a cloudier history. The saint's day was established in 496 as a celebration of his martyrdom more than 200 years earlier. Not until 1493 did the legend of Valentine helping persecuted lovers appear. Why a Roman Catholic saint's day gained popular appeal in 1840s America—a time of widespread prejudice against Roman Catholics—is unclear. However, it is known that mass-produced Valentine cards found a market as early as 1847, when Esther Howland of Worcester, Massachusetts, started selling lacy, sentimental confections.

The death of sentimentality is evident in the sudden rise of Halloween. The National Retail Federation calls it the sixth largest holiday for retail spending, worth about $5 billion in 2006, with $1.8 billion spent on costumes alone. Party City says it is the second largest holiday for decorating, trailing only Christmas, thanks to the popularity of plastic bats and faux gravestones. Two-thirds of all Americans attend Halloween parties, with participation reaching 85 percent among 18-to 24-year-olds.

The other popular holiday for dressing up and letting down inhibitions is Mardi Gras, the Fat Tuesday that precedes the start of Lent, which in turn leads to Easter. Lent—a period of prayer, fasting, and alms giving before Easter—would seem to be the last event that could attract retail sales. The Roman Catholic requirement to eat no meat on Lenten Fridays makes this the season for restaurants to promote their fish menus. KFC has gone so far as to request that the Pope bless its new fish sandwich.

# ▶ A Short Story ▶

## Turkey

Turkey is the most common main dish of a Thanksgiving dinner, to the point where Thanksgiving is sometimes colloquially called "Turkey Day." In 2006, American turkey growers were expected to raise 270 million turkeys, to be processed into five billion pounds of turkey meat valued at almost $8 billion, with one third of all turkey consumption occurring in the Thanksgiving-

Christmas season, and a per capita consumption of almost 18 pounds (8.2 kg). The Broad Breasted White turkey is particularly bred for Thanksgiving dinner and similar large feasts; its large size (specimens can grow to over 40 pounds) and meat content make it ideal for such situations, although the breed must be artificially bred and suffers from health problems due to its size.

Most Thanksgiving turkeys are stuffed with a bread-based mixture and roasted. Sage is the traditional herb added to the stuffing (also called dressing if NOT cooked inside the bird), along with chopped celery, carrots, and onions. Other ingredients, such as chopped chestnuts or other tree nuts, crumbled sausage or bacon, cranberries, raisins, or apples, may be added to stuffing. Deep-fried turkey is rising in popularity due to its shorter preparation time, but carries safety risks.

The consumption of turkey on Thanksgiving is so ingrained in American culture that each year since 1947, the National Turkey Federation has presented a live turkey to the President of the United States prior to each Thanksgiving. These turkeys were initially slaughtered and eaten for the President's Thanksgiving dinner; since 1989, the presented turkeys have typically been given a mock "pardon" to great fanfare and sent to a park to live out the rest of their usually short natural lives.

### ▬ *Exercises* ▬

【Fill in the Blanks】

1. The first Thanksgiving Day was celebrated by the English settlers in Plymouth, _____.

2. _____ and _____ are symbols most frequently associated with Easter.

3. Holidays are days that are set apart for public, _____ or special observances.

4. _____ is America's most important patriotic holiday, the birthday of the nation.

5. _____ is an annual day of thanks for the blessings people have enjoyed during the year.

【Multiple Choices】

1. Independence Day of the United Stated is on _____.

    A. February 12th    B. July 4th    C. November 11th    D. May 1st

2. People still remember _____ 's famous words "United we stand, divided we fall".

    A. Martin Luther King           B. George Washington

    C. Rock Feller                  D. Abraham Lincoln

3. Eater Sunday comes from the ancient _____ festival of Spring Sun.

    A. Norwegian        B. Sweden    C. Indian        D. English

4. _____ is a day for lovers.

    A. Easter Sunday                B. Veterans' Day

    C. Valentine's Day              D. Halloween

5. What day it is Thanksgiving Day?

    A. The Fourth Thursday of November.

    B. The First Thursday of November.

    C. The Fourth Sunday of November.

    D. The First Sunday of November.

【Discussion】

1. What are the basic reasons for the establishment of holidays in the U.S.?

2. What are the holidays relevant to Christmas Day?

# Unit 16

# Food

"Let's grab a bite to eat." This typical American expression suggests a host of unsavory connotations. Children are chastised for grabbing. There is a sense of lawlessness and a certain impropriety about grabbing things. Grabbing is not polite, but millions of Americans are grabbing a bite to eat every day. Grabbing is what is done on the run. There is a kind of national fast food cuisine to cater to all these people on the run, but fast food is just part of the story. Contrary to their portrayals in films, Americans are not always running. In fact, their expenditures on fast food are a relatively small portion of their total food expenditures.

The same transportation and food handling systems that helped to create a national fast food cuisine have also blurred the lines among regional cuisines. It is not at all unusual for Maine lobsters to be served in restaurants in California or Rhode Island quahogs to show up in chowder in Arizona. Traditional American cuisine is, however, regional, based on what is available. It is differentiated generally by method and by national origin. The Germans and the English had the biggest effect on the development of American cooking because they represented the largest groups of America's first immigrants. It should not be forgotten, however, that the United States began its existence as 13 English colonies inhabited mostly by English men and women .The development of the jambalaya that became called American food can be seen, therefore, as a gradual liberation from simple English home cooking. Midwest cuisine is based heavily on the movement and settlement first of Germans and then Scandinavians. Southern cuisine is inextricably mixed with the legacy of slavery, as black slaves over time turned high-table

English plantation cooking into flavorful dishes no longer English or African, but completely American. Southwestern cuisine can no longer be broken down into its component native Indian, Mexican, Spanish, and Anglo components. California, with its incredible ethnic diversity, has developed a regional cuisine that is consciously based on fusing the culinary arts of various cultures with locally produced goods. The Pacific Northwest is a developing cuisine but is most certainly based on regionally available fresh food.

"That's American as apple pie." This often heard American expression is meant to refer to anything an American thinks is really American. The fact is, of course, that apple pie is not American at all. Recipes for apple pies showed up in Elizabethan England and were even stowed away on the ships bringing the first colonists to American shores. Typically, apple pies became so ubiquitous that Americans appropriated them as their own. To most Americans, apple pie is a national emblem of American cuisine. Yet in spite of the American preoccupation with uniformity in food—a Big Mac is a Big Mac in Boston, Kansas City, and Los Angeles—even apple pies are susceptible to regional variation. Germans and Amish in Pennsylvania may toss in some sour cream and raisins or ice the top pastry layer. In Massachusetts, some cranberries may find themselves baked with the apples. Apple chiffon pie is popular in upstate New York. In Illinois, apples and pumpkin might be pureed together in a pie. An old California recipe cooked the apples first and laid them on a bed of caramel sauce before baking.

The case of the lowly bean illustrates even better the regional nature of American cuisine. Beans, no matter the variety, have always been a staple in American diets. Boston has proudly accepted the appellation "Bean Town" since the 1700s thanks to its great northern baked beans flavored with brown sugar and molasses. In south Texas, however, barbequed baked pink beans get spiced up with chilies. In Vermont, baked navy beans get a treatment of apples and maple syrup. Hoppin' John in the southern Low Country pairs rice with black-eyed peas and ham. In the Southwest, Pueblo Indians combined chorizos, a legacy of Spain, beef, hot peppers, cumin, corn, and tomatoes with Anasazi beans for a local delicacy.

So what does it mean to have an American meal? There is no recipe for cooking the American way. American cooking, like American life, is an individual effort in which innovation and efficiency are prized. Quite simply, American food is what Americans cook and eat. It is food appropriated from the cultures of the people who lived or came there and, in most all cases, changed to fit local circumstance, taste, and the means of mass production.

In 2002, each American ate (per capita consumption) 64.5 pounds of beef, 48.2 pounds of pork, 56.8 pounds of chicken, 15.6 pounds of fish and shellfish, 180 eggs, 885.31 pounds of dairy products, 30.5 pounds of cheese (topped by American at 12.8 pounds, followed by Italian at 12.4 pounds), 26.4 pounds of frozen dairy products, 191.3 pounds of flour and cereal products, 63.2 pounds of sugar, 125.6 pounds of fresh fruit and 146.0 pounds of processed fruit, 193.4 pounds of fresh vegetables (potatoes in first place at 45.0 pounds, and lettuce in second place at 22.4 pounds), and 208.6 pounds of processed vegetables. Americans also per capita drank 23.6 gallons of coffee, 7.8 gallons of tea, 21.9 gallons of milk, 8.0 gallons of fruit juice, 21.8 gallons of beer, 2.1 gallons of wine, and 1.3 gallons of distilled liquor.

Food is big business in America, the birthplace of casual dining. In 2006, there were about 925,000 restaurants in the United States, which means there is roughly one restaurant for every 300 people, and 70 percent of them are single-restaurant small businesses. More than 50 percent of American adults have worked at one time in the restaurant industry. Estimates are that Americans spent $511 billion in these eating and drinking establishments, which have 12.5 million employees, thus making the restaurant industry second only to government in number of workers. On a given day, 130,000,000 Americans visit a restaurant for a meal or a snack, and they spend, on average, $2,434 per household, or $974 per person per year, eating out. Americans spent 47 percent of their total food money in restaurants in 2006, up dramatically from only 25 percent in 1955. Americans like to eat out. Sixty-six percent of them agree that they can get flavorful food eating out that cannot easily be duplicated at home. Americans spend about $165 billion a year at full-service restaurants. Snack and non-alcoholic beverage bars pull in almost $17 billion, cafeterias and buffets, another $5.3 billion. Bars and taverns have annual revenues of more than $15.2 billion. Hotel restaurants bring in nearly $25 billion a year. Business and leisure travel help to fuel restaurant sales, as do major holidays. Mother's Day, for example, brings 62 percent of those celebrating the occasion with special meals into restaurants. Many will go out for more than one meal. Twenty-two percent go for breakfast, 51 percent for lunch or brunch, and 59 percent for dinner. Fast-food eating places account for over $134 billion per year of Americans' food expenditures.

All-you-can-eat restaurants and buffets are popular in America. Needless to say, Nouvelle cuisine, as it morphed into American cooking as the new American cuisine, was not a hit with the typical hungry American. The problem was not fresh ingredients, or even the lack of rich sauces (gravy to Americans).

Full-service restaurants run the gamut from tiny little independent neighborhood eating establishments to themed, casual dining chain restaurants like Chipotle Mexican Grill, Outback Steak House, Olive Garden, and Red Lobster. In 2006, only 15 restaurants in all the United States earned that distinction. New York City had four; the San Francisco area, three; Atlanta, two; Los Angeles, Chicago, and Philadelphia, one each. The others were located in Washington, Virginia, Summerville, South Carolina, and Kennebunkport, Maine.

What do ordinary Americans order when they go to restaurants on a typical day? The top 10 selections for men in descending order according to one survey were a hamburger, French fries, pizza, a breakfast sandwich, a side salad, eggs, doughnuts, hash brown potatoes, Chinese food, and a main salad. Women ordered French fries, a hamburger, pizza, a side salad, a chicken sandwich, a breakfast sandwich, a main salad, Chinese food, and rice.

Hamburgers, sold in the billions each year from ubiquitous franchises (McDonald's, Burger King, and Wendy's are, in order, the largest), bars and taverns, and county and state fairs—anywhere there are Americans—are the quintessential American food. Hamburgers are also featured at most backyard cookouts, tailgate parties, picnics, and sports events. Most of the beef consumed in America is in the form of ground beef-hamburger. American ingenuity has elevated the simple hamburger to a gastronomic art form. The hamburger chains have attempted to brand their burgers by charbroiling them, flame-broiling them, steaming them with onions, and grilling them; by shaping them round, square, and triangular; and by heaping them with varieties of condiments including lettuce, tomatoes, mayonnaise, special sauces, secret sauces, salad dressings, onions, peppers, chilies, mustard, and ketchup, not to exhaust the list. Many local restaurants claim to have the best hamburger in town. Indeed, the variations are endless. A hamburger steak, ground sir-loin, may be at the pinnacle of the hamburger hierarchy, but the American meatloaf (a baked loaf of ground beef and pork and spices of choice) is a basic American concoction that has reached such gustatory heights that famous American-born French chef Julia Child called it American pâté.

Ordering a hamburger and fries is like ordering ham and eggs or milk and cookies—they just go together naturally in the American mind. French fries, as the name implies, are not American in origin (they are Belgian, as the name does not imply). Neither, of course, is pizza, which Americans have transformed from a simple Italian tomato bread starter into a gigantic complete meal. Bigger is always better; Americans eat around 100 acres of pizza every day. Ninety-three percent of all Americans eat at least one pizza a month; about 3 billion pizzas are sold every year. Like the hamburger, the pizza has been subjected to American inventiveness. There are nearly 70,000 pizzerias in the United States, 64.3 percent of which are independents, but they accounted for a bit fewer than 50 percent of total U.S. sales of almost $31 billion. The top 25 pizzeria chains with nearly 25,000 stores account for just over 50 percent of total U.S. sales. Pizza Hut, the largest chain, alone accounts for over 17 percent of all sales. They, too, are round and square, small and large, and can have just about anything on them. There are Hawaiian pizzas (pineapple and ham), Mexican pizzas, barbeque pizzas, white pizzas (no tomato sauce), fish pizzas, vegetable pizzas, Cajun pizzas, eggplant pizzas, venison pizzas, duck pizzas, and even breakfast pizzas, with peanut butter and jelly or bacon and eggs. Sixty-two percent of Americans want meat on their pizza, and 36 percent of all pizzas ordered have pepperoni on them. Other traditional favorite ingredients are mushrooms, extra cheese, sausage, green peppers, and onions.

There are about an equal number of Italian and Chinese full-service restaurants in America. Among limited service restaurants, mostly carryout establishments, Mexican restaurants outnumber Chinese restaurants seven to five and Italian restaurants seven to two. All together, there are more than 40,000 each of Mexican and Chinese restaurants in the United States. Italian, Chinese, and Mexican cuisines have been completely incorporated into what might be called the category of typical American food, what Americans like to eat, and they eat a lot of it. Spaghetti and meatballs, egg rolls, and tacos are standard fare eating out and at home. If college students can be thought of as future trendsetters, there is no going back to old-time plain American cooking. When asked what their favorite cuisines were, 95 percent liked Italian; 90 percent liked Mexican; and 83 percent liked Chinese.

Many have decried the fact that the traditional American sit-down family meal has gone the way of tintype and typewriters. Most parents work outside the home, and kids have busy schedules filled with athletic activities, events, and other after-school obligations, to which they must be shuttled back and forth. Eating on the go is the new American meal tradition. There is little time for food preparation and precious little time to gulp it down. America has produced new generations for whom comfort food in later life is a box of macaroni and cheese, which they learned to make in a microwave at the age of five, mostly out of necessity. So what are Americans eating at home?

A trip to the grocery store, where shelf space is at a premium and grocers give space only to what sells fast, lends some understanding. Fresh fruit and vegetables get half an aisle, as do fresh meats (a lot of space for hamburger) and breads. Soft drinks (Coke, Pepsi, and tens of variations) and snacks (potato chips, tortilla chips, peanuts, etc.) get an entire aisle. Juices and various kinds of sport drinks have nearly half an aisle, and canned vegetables get half that. Soups, in cans, in ready-to-eat containers, and in boxes, get about a quarter aisles. Fruit, in cans, but mostly in ready-to-eat containers, get about a quarter of an aisle, but cookies and crackers get more space. There seems to be a lot of boxes: rows of cake mixes, bread mixes, muffin mixes, and cookie mixes. Cereal, the all-American breakfast food, gets a full side of an aisle. Even more impressive is the space given to boxes of rice, potatoes, and pasta. Boxes of potatoes may seem unnatural, but by just adding water, milk, and butter or margarine, and a few minutes of cooking, a variety of potato dishes can be created quickly. Rice gets some space, but not much in its pure form. Small boxes of rice with flavor packets tucked into the box get quite a bit of space. Nearly an entire row is filled with pasta in all its sizes and shapes, accompanied by jars of prepared spaghetti sauce, clam sauce, and Alfredo sauce. The Mexican food section is growing, but the Italian foods, as under-stood, coopted, and transformed by Americans, are the space winner. Busy American cooks can also go to another aisle to choose from nearly half a row of boxes of macaroni and cheese, pasta salad, and pasta dishes. In fact, in the continuing tribute to American food as the ultimate fusion cuisine, a chicken quesadilla flavor pasta is now available in a box. Those who find that to be too much fusion can always rely on Hamburger Helper available in several flavors. Just fry the hamburger, add the flavor packet and pasta and some water, and you have an American meal.

Six times a month, the typical American sits down to a heated up frozen meal. In 2003, Americans spent over ＄6 billion on frozen dinners and entrees. In total, they spent ＄29.2 billion on frozen foods. Frozen vegetable sales of ＄2.8 billion, which included ＄858 million of frozen potatoes, nearly equaled frozen pizza sales of ＄2.74 billion. Sales of ice cream, which many Americans would con-sider a homegrown invention, came to ＄4.8 billion.

Wine is sold in some 3,000 grocery stores as well as other stores across the nation. U.S. wine consumption has been increasing steadily since 1991 and across age and ethnic lines. Many Americans now consider wine to be a requirement of a good meal, especially in a good restaurant, but it is also served at home on special occasions. Wine is a staple at parties, often replacing hard liquor. In 2005, wine sales in the United States totaled 703 million gallons, valued at $ 26 billion. Table wines accounted for most of the sales at 619 million gallons; champagne and sparkling wines came to only 30 million gallons. The remainder was dessert wines. Amazingly, California wines took a 63 percent market share of all wines sold. California produced 532 million gallons of wine in 2005, of which 441 million gallons were sold in the United States. Premium wines, defined as $ 7 or more per bottle, were 66 percent of revenues, and everyday wines, below $ 7 per bottle, constituted the remainder. U.S. wine exports of 101 million gallons were 95 percent California wines. While wine is grown all across America, there can be little doubt that California wines are the ones that have made American wines respectable around the globe.

Americans like American beer. In fact, July is American beer month. Breweries were first licensed in New England in 1637. Beer is now an $ 83 billion business. In 2005, domestic beer sales of 178.8 million barrels (a barrel equals 31 U.S. gallons) dwarfed sales of 25.7 million barrels for imported beers. The large brewers, such as Anheuser Busch, with its flagship Budweiser brand, dominate the domestic beer market. That company alone accounts for around half of all domestic beer sales. The big brewers—also including Miller, Coors, and Pabst—have attempted to bolster their sales by catering to weight-conscious beer drinkers with light and low-carbohydrate brews, which are overtaking traditional lagers in sales. There is, however, another concurrent trend in American brewing filled by America's 1,415 craft breweries, which are turning out multiflavored and full-bodied 100 percent malt beers. These regional craft breweries, contract breweries, microbreweries, and brewpubs together are a $ 4. 3 billion dollar business that produces about 7 million barrels annually and takes a 3.42 percent share of the American beer market. That is not much compared to the non-craft domestic brewers' 84.14 percent of the market or even imported beers' share of 12.43 percent, but craft brewers are providing Americans with an alternative to what critics have been known to call insipid American beer.

America's original contribution to the family of distilled spirits was inspired by a native American food staple combined with Scotch-Irish immigrant distilling know-how and then given a French name. It even caused a rebellion in 1794 in Pennsylvania that George Washington himself had to put down after the federal government tried to tax it. Bourbon whiskey, the old red eye, rotgut, and firewater of the Wild West, was distinguished from other whiskies by the use of corn in the mash. Corn was preferred in southern whiskey making, rather than the rye that was used prevalently in the North. Americans soon came to favor the smoothness of the corn-based whisky. By 1784, commercial distilleries were operating in Kentucky, and Bourbon County, Kentucky, became the center of bourbon whiskey production in the United States, thus lending its name to the product. Today, regulations require that bourbon be at least 51 percent corn and aged for not less than two years in new charred barrels. Tennessee whiskey, a distinct classification from bourbon, has an additional requirement of being filtered through sugar maple charcoal. Moonshine is the source of much American humor and a stepping off point for story lines that celebrate individual freedom over government regulation.

Alcoholic beverages made up only about 13 percent of each American's total consumption of 192 gallons of liquids in 2004. In the country that made Coke and Pepsi internationally known trademarks, combined diet and non-diet carbonated soft drinks alone counted for 28 percent of consumption. That is about 52 gallons a year for each American, for which Americans spent about $66 billion. Far behind in second place, bottled water was only 12.4 percent. Curiously, milk, coffee, beer, and all others (including tap water, vegetable juices, and sports drinks) each account for between 11 percent and 12 percent of liquid consumption per year. Fruit juices came in at 7.6 percent and tea at 4.4 percent. Americans have about 450 soft drinks from which to choose that are produced in around 400 plants. The most efficient plants can produce 2,000 cans of soda per minute per line to satisfy the demand for more than 68 billion cans a year. Only 23 percent of soft drinks are fountain dispensed, rather than packaged.

Americans consume legumes in large amounts, and in the case of peanuts, without knowing they are eating them, since most think they are nuts like walnuts or pecans. Peanuts came to the United States via South America and are grown today mostly on small farms in the South that average 100 acres. Each American eats over six pounds of peanuts—a favorite snack food both roasted and salted and great with beer and cocktails—and products made from peanut butter a year. Most peanuts are used to make peanut butter, which was patented by Harvey Kellogg in 1895, who also brought corn flakes to the world, but it was first sold at the 1904 St. Louis World's Fair. By 1908, it was being produced commercially. The annual consumption of peanut butter, on which Americans spend $800 million a year, is enough to make 10 billion peanut butter and jelly sandwiches (PB & Js). Peanut butter and jelly sandwiches—soft white bread, peanut butter, and Concord grape (preferably) jelly—have a place in every young student's lunch pail. The typical young American will have eaten 1,500 PB & Js before graduating from high school.

In America's schizophrenic lifestyle, there is one thing that brings families together: the backyard cookout, which usually takes place on weekends with family and friends. For Americans in New England and the Midwest, it is a celebration of the outdoors after being shut in the house all winter and liberation from the kitchen. Most families have outdoor grills—some cheap and serviceable charcoal grills, others gas-fired and quite elaborate. Grilling the meat—spareribs, steaks, hamburgers, hot dogs, pork chops—is typically the man's job for some primordial reason. Back in the kitchen, the woman pre-pares (or opens the containers of) the staples of the cookout: coleslaw (a gift to America from early Dutch settlers), macaroni salad, and baked beans. The red ketchup and yellow mustard, the jar of pickles, and some sliced onions and tomatoes are placed on the backyard picnic table with the hotdog and hamburger buns, the beer and soft drinks are in the cooler, and the party is under way. Ice cream, brownies, and watermelon are for dessert.

## ▶ A Short Story ◀

### Burger King

Burger King (BK) is an American global chain of hamburger fast food restaurants. Headquartered in the unincorporated area of Miami-Dade County, Florida, the company was founded in 1953 as Insta-Burger King, a Jacksonville, Florida-based restaurant chain. After Insta-Burger King ran into financial difficulties in 1954, its two Miami-based franchisees David Edgerton and James McLamore purchased the company and renamed it "Burger King." Over the next half-century, the company would change hands four times, with its third set of owners, a partnership of TPG Capital, Bain Capital, and Goldman Sachs Capital Partners, taking it public in 2002. In late 2010, 3G Capital of Brazil acquired a majority stake in the company, in a deal valued at US $3.26 billion. The new owners promptly initiated a restructuring of the company to reverse its fortunes. 3G, along with partner Berkshire Hathaway, eventually merged the company with the Canadian-based doughnut chain Tim Hortons, under the auspices of a new Canadian-based parent company named Restaurant Brands International.

The 1970s were the "Golden Age" of the company's advertising, but beginning in the early-1980s, Burger King advertising began losing focus. A series of less successful advertising campaigns created by a procession of advertising agencies continued for the next two decades. In 2003, Burger King hired the Miami-based advertising agency Crispin Porter + Bogusky (CP+B), who completely reorganized its advertising with a series of new campaigns centered on a redesigned Burger King character nicknamed "The King," accompanied by a new online presence. While highly successful, some of CP+B's commercials were derided for perceived sexism or cultural insensitivity. Burger King's new owner, 3G Capital, later terminated the relationship with CP+B in 2011 and moved its advertising to McGarryBowen, to begin a new product-oriented campaign with expanded demographic targeting.

Burger King's menu has expanded from a basic offering of burgers, French fries, sodas, and milkshakes to a larger and more diverse set of products. In 1957, the "Whopper" became the first major addition to the menu, and it has become Burger King's signature product since. Conversely, BK has introduced many products, which failed to catch hold in the marketplace. Some of these failures in the United States have seen success in foreign markets, where BK has also tailored its menu for regional tastes. From 2002 to 2010, Burger King aggressively targeted the 18-34 male demographic with larger products that often carried correspondingly large amounts of unhealthy fats and trans-fats. This tactic would eventually damage the company's financial underpinnings, and cast a negative pall on its earnings. Beginning in 2011, the company began to move away from its previous male-oriented menu and introduce new menu items, product reformulations and packaging, as part of its current owner 3G Capital's restructuring plans of the company.

As of December 31st, 2016, Burger King reported it had 15,738 outlets in 100 countries. Of these, 47.5% are in the United States and 99.5% are privately owned and operated, with its new owners moving to an almost entirely franchised model in 2013. BK has historically used several variations of franchising to expand its operations. The manner in which the company licenses its franchisees varies depending on the region, with some regional franchises, known as master franchises, responsible for selling franchise sub-licenses on the company's behalf. Burger King's relationship with its franchises has not always been harmonious. Occasional spats between the two have caused numerous issues, and in several instances, the company's and its licensees' relations have degenerated into precedent-setting court cases. Burger King's Australian franchise Hungry Jack's is the only franchise to operate under a different name, due to a trademark dispute and a series of legal cases between the two.

### ▪▪▪ Exercises ▪▪▪

【Fill in the Blanks】

1. Today the American food is very popular in _____.

2. The same transportation and food handling systems that helped to create a national _____ food cuisine have also blurred the lines among cuisines.

3. In Massachusetts, some cranberries may find themselves baked with the _____.

4. Food is big business in American, the _____ of casual dining.

5. Wine is sold in some _____ grocery stores as well as other stores across the nation.

【Multiple Choices】

1. In 2006, there were about _____ restaurants in the U.S.
    A. 920,000        B. 920, 500        C. 925,000        D. 925,500

2. Americans eat around _____ acres of pizza every day.
    A. 200        B. 100        C. 150        D. 180

3. There are about an equal number of _____ full-service restaurants in American.
    A. Italian and Britain            B. Italian and China
    C. Britain and Canada            D. Britain and China

4. California Produced _____ million gallons of wine in 2005.
    A. 532        B. 523        C. 512        D. 531

5. Which of the following helps theorize the concept of Fraternity?
    A. Karl Marx.            B. Ralph Ellison.
    C. Franklin Roosevelt.            D. James Baldwin.

【Discussion】

1. What are the main ingredients of American food?

2. What are the regional features of American food?

3. How can you describe the history of wine in the U.S.?

## Unit 17

# Literature

American literature is the literature written or produced in the area of the United States and its preceding colonies. During its early history, America was a series of British colonies on the eastern coast of the present-day United States. Therefore, its literary tradition begins as linked to the broader tradition of English literature. However, unique American characteristics and the breadth of its production usually now cause it to be considered a separate path and tradition.

The New England colonies were the center of early American literature. The revolutionary period contained political writings by Samuel Adams, Benjamin Franklin and Thomas Paine. In the post-war period, Thomas Jefferson's *United States Declaration of Independence* solidified his status as a key American writer. It was in the late 18th and early 19th centuries that the nation's first novels were published. With the War of 1812 and an increasing desire to produce uniquely American literature and culture, a number of key new literary figures emerged. In 1836, Ralph Waldo Emerson (1803–1882) started a movement known as Transcendentalism. Henry David Thoreau (1817–1862) wrote *Walden*, which urges resistance to the dictates of organized society. The political conflict surrounding abolitionism inspired the writings of William Lloyd Garrison and Harriet Beecher Stowe in her world-famous *Uncle Tom's Cabin*. These efforts were supported by the continuation of the slave narrative autobiography, of which the best known example from this period was Frederick Douglass's *Narrative of the Life of Frederick Douglass, an American Slave*.

American poetry reached a peak in the early-to-mid-20th century, with such noted writers as Wallace Stevens, T. S. Eliot, Robert Frost, Ezra Pound, Hart Crane, and E. E. Cummings. Mark Twain (the pen name used by Samuel Langhorne Clemens, 1835-1910) was the first major American writer to be born away from the East Coast. Henry James (1843-1916) was notable for novels like *The Turn of the Screw.* At the beginning of the 20th century, American novelists included Edith Wharton (1862-1937), Stephen Crane (1871-1900), Theodore Dreiser (1871-1945), and Jack London (1876-1916). Experimentation in style and form is seen in the works of Gertrude Stein (1874-1946).

American writers expressed disillusionment following World War I. The stories and novels of F. Scott Fitzgerald (1896-1940) captured the mood of the 1920s, and John Dos Passos wrote about the war. Ernest Hemingway (1899-1961) became notable for *The Sun Also Rises* and *A Farewell to Arms*; in 1954, he won the Nobel Prize in Literature. William Faulkner (1897-1962) is notable for novels like *The Sound and the Fury*. American drama attained international status only in the 1920s and 1930s, with the works of Eugene O'Neill, who won four Pulitzer Prizes and the Nobel Prize. In the middle of the 20th century, American drama was dominated by the work of playwrights Tennessee Williams and Arthur Miller, as well as by the maturation of the American musical.

Depression era writers included John Steinbeck (1902-1968), notable for his novel *The Grapes of Wrath*. Henry Miller assumed a unique place in American literature in the 1930s when his semi-autobiographical novels were banned from the U.S. From the end of World War II up until, roughly, the late 1960s and early 1970s saw the publication of some of the most popular works in American history such as *To Kill a Mockingbird* by Harper Lee. America's involvement in World War II influenced the creation of works such as Norman Mailer's *The Naked and the Dead* (1948), Joseph Heller's *Catch-22* (1961) and Kurt Vonnegut Jr.'s *Slaughterhouse-Five* (1969). John Updike was notable for his novel *Rabbit, Run* (1960). Philip Roth explored Jewish identity in American society. From the early 1970s to the present day the most important literary movement has been postmodernism and the flowering of literature by ethnic minority writers.

**Contemporary American literature**

Though its exact parameters remain debatable, from the early 1970s to the present day the most salient literary movement has been postmodernism. Thomas Pynchon, a seminal practitioner of the form, drew in his work on modernist fixtures such as temporal distortion, unreliable narrators, and internal monologue and coupled them with distinctly postmodern techniques. In 1973, he published *Gravity's Rainbow*, a leading work in this genre, which won the National Book Award and was unanimously nominated for the Pulitzer Prize for Fiction that year. His other major works include his debut, *V.* (1963), *The Crying of Lot 49* (1966), *Mason & Dixon* (1997), and *Against the Day* (2006).

Toni Morrison, one of the American recipients of the Nobel Prize for Literature, writing in a distinctive lyrical prose style, published her controversial debut novel, *The Bluest Eye*, to widespread critical acclaim in 1970. Coming on the heels of the signing of the *Civil Rights Act of 1965*, the novel includes an elaborate description of incestuous rape and explores the conventions of beauty established by a historically racist society, painting a portrait of a self-immolating black family in search of beauty in whiteness. Since then, Morrison has experimented with lyric fantasy, *Song of Solomon* (1977) and *Beloved* (1987), for which she was awarded the Pulitzer Prize for Fiction; along these lines, critic Harold Bloom has drawn favorable comparisons to Virginia Woolf, and the Nobel committee to "Faulkner and to the Latin American tradition [of magical realism]." *Beloved* was chosen in a 2006 survey conducted by the *New York Times* as the most important work of fiction of the last 25 years.

Writing in a lyrical, flowing style that eschews excessive use of the comma and semicolon, recalling William Faulkner and Ernest Hemingway in equal measure, Cormac McCarthy's body of work seizes on the literary traditions of several regions of the United States and spans multiple genres. He writes in the Southern Gothic aesthetic in his distinctly Faulknerian 1965 debut, *The Orchard Keeper*, and *Suttree* (1979); in the Epic Western tradition, with grotesquely drawn characters and symbolic narrative turns reminiscent of Melville; in *Blood Meridian* (1985), which Harold Bloom styled "the greatest single book since Faulkner's *As I Lay Dying*," calling the character of Judge Holden "short of *Moby Dick*, the most monstrous apparition in all of American literature"; in a much more pastoral tone in his celebrated *Border Trilogy* (1992-1998) of bildungsromans, including *All the Pretty Horses* (1992), winner of the National Book Award; and in the post-apocalyptic genre in the Pulitzer Prize-winning *The Road* (2007). His novels are noted for achieving both commercial and critical success, several of his works having been adapted to film.

Don DeLillo, who rose to literary prominence with the publication of his 1985 novel, *White Noise*, began his writing career in 1971 with Americana. He is listed by Harold Bloom as being among the preeminent contemporary American writers, in the company of such figures as Philip Roth, Cormac McCarthy, and Thomas Pynchon. His 1997 novel *Underworld* is a gargantuan work chronicling American life through and immediately after the Cold War and examining with equal depth subjects as various as baseball and nuclear weapons. It is generally agreed upon to be his masterpiece and was the runner-up in a survey asking writers to identify the most important work of fiction of the last 25 years. Among his other important novels are *Libra* (1988), *Mao II* (1991) and *Falling Man* (2007).

Seizing on the distinctly postmodern techniques of digression, narrative fragmentation and elaborate symbolism, and strongly influenced by the works of Thomas Pynchon, David Foster Wallace began his writing career with *The Broom of the System*, published to moderate acclaim in 1987. His second novel, *Infinite Jest* (1997), is a futuristic portrait of America and a playful critique of the media-saturated nature of American life. It has been consistently ranked among the most important works of the 20th century, and his final novel, unfinished at the time of his death, *The Pale King* (2011), has garnered much praise and attention. In addition to his novels, he also authored three acclaimed short story collections: *Girl with Curious Hair* (1989), *Brief Interviews with Hideous Men* (1999) and *Oblivion : Stories* (2004).

Jonathan Franzen, Wallace's friend and contemporary, rose to prominence after the 2001 publication of his National Book Award-winning third novel, *The Corrections*. He began his writing career in 1988 with the well-received *The Twenty-Seventh City*, a novel centering on his native St. Louis, but did not gain national attention until the publication of his essay, "Perchance to Dream," in *Harper's Magazine*. It discussed the cultural role of the writer in the new millennium through the prism of his own frustrations. *The Corrections*, a tragicomedy about the disintegrating Lambert family, has been called "the literary phenomenon of [its] decade" and was ranked as one of the greatest novels of the past century. In 2010, he published *Freedom* to great critical acclaim.

Other notable writers at the turn of the century include Michael Chabon, whose Pulitzer Prize-winning *The Amazing Adventures of Kavalier & Clay* (2000) tells the story of two friends, Joe Kavalier and Sam Clay, as they rise through the ranks of the comics industry in its heyday; Denis Johnson, whose 2007 novel *Tree of Smoke* about falsified intelligence during Vietnam both won the National Book Award and was a finalist for the Pulitzer Prize for Fiction and was called by critic Michiko Kakutani "one of the classic works of literature produced by [the Vietnam War]"; and Louise Erdrich, whose 2008 novel *The Plague of Doves*, a distinctly Faulknerian, polyphonic examination of the tribal experience set against the backdrop of murder in the fictional town of Pluto, North Dakota, was nominated for the Pulitzer Prize, and her 2012 novel *The Round House*, which builds on the same themes, was awarded the 2012 National Book Award.

Nobel Prize in Literature winners (American authors):

1930: Sinclair Lewis (novelist)

1936: Eugene O'Neill (playwright)

1938: Pearl S. Buck (biographer and novelist)

1948: T. S. Eliot (poet and playwright)

1949: William Faulkner (novelist)

1954: Ernest Hemingway (novelist)

1962: John Steinbeck (novelist)

1976: Saul Bellow (novelist)

1978：Isaac Bashevis Singer (novelist, wrote in Yiddish)

1987：Joseph Brodsky (poet and essayist, wrote in English and Russian)

1993：Toni Morrison (novelist)

2016：Bob Dylan (songwriter)

## ▶ A Short Story ◀

### Bob Dylan

Bob Dylan is an American singer, songwriter, musician, painter, and writer. He has been influential in popular music and culture for more than five decades. Much of his most celebrated works dates from the 1960s, when he became a reluctant "voice of a generation" with songs such as *Blowing in the Wind* and *The Times They Are a-Changing*, which became anthems for the Civil Rights Movement and anti-war movement. Leaving behind his initial base in the American folk music revival, his six-minute single "Like a Rolling Stone", recorded in 1965, enlarged the range of popular music.

Dylan's lyrics incorporate a wide range of political, social, philosophical, and literary influences. They defied existing pop music conventions and appealed to the burgeoning counterculture. Initially inspired by the performances of Little Richard and the songwriting of Woody Guthrie, Robert Johnson, and Hank Williams, Dylan has amplified and personalized musical genres. His recording career, spanning more than 50 years, has explored the traditions in American song—from folk, blues, and country to gospel, rock and roll, and rockabilly to English, Scottish, and Irish folk music, embracing even jazz and the Great American Songbook. Dylan performs with guitar, keyboards, and harmonica. Backed by a changing lineup of musicians, he has toured steadily since the late 1980s on what has been dubbed the Never Ending Tour. His accomplishments as a recording artist and performer have been central to his career, but his songwriting is considered his greatest contribution. Since 1994, Dylan has also published seven books of drawings and paintings, and his work has been exhibited in major art galleries.

As a musician, Dylan has sold more than 100 million records, making him one of the best-selling artists of all time. He has also received numerous awards including eleven Grammy Awards, a Golden Globe Award, and an Academy Award. Dylan has been inducted into the Rock and Roll Hall of Fame, Minnesota Music Hall of Fame, Nashville Songwriters Hall of Fame, and Songwriters Hall of Fame. The Pulitzer Prize jury in 2008 awarded him a special citation for "his profound impact on popular music and American culture, marked by lyrical compositions of extraordinary poetic power." In May 2012, Dylan received the Presidential Medal of Freedom from President Barack Obama. In 2016, he was awarded the Nobel Prize in Literature "for having created new poetic expressions within the great American song tradition."

## ▪▪▪ Exercises ▪▪▪

【Fill in the Blanks】

1. *Rip Van Winkle* is a story based on an old _____ folk tale.

2. F. Scott Fitzgerald's novel _____ was about youth's golden dream turning to disappointment.

3. Richard Wright wrote the novel _____, and Ralph Ellison wrote the novel _____.

4. _____ won the Nobel Prize for Literature in 1993, the first Afro-American writer to receive this honor.

5. Mark Twain's _____ is considered the greatest novel in American literature.

【Multiple Choices】

1. Whitman's poetry has the following characteristics except _____.

    A. fragmented haunting images

    B. long irregular lines

    C. celebrating the American spirit

    D. free-flowing structure

2. Mark Twain's works are characterized by the following except _____.

A. sense of humor     B. egotism     C. jokes     D. tall tales

3. _____ was mainly interested in writing about Americans living in Europe.

 A. Henry James                    B. Mark Twain

 C. William Dean Howells           D. Stephen Crane

4. _____ was not written by Hemingway.

 A. *Light in August*              B. *The Sun Also Rises*

 C. *A Farewell to Arms*           D. *For Whom the Bell Tolls*

5. Which of the following is not an African-American author?

 A. Richard Wright.                B. Alan Ginsberg.

 C. James Baldwin.                 D. Ralph Ellison.

【Discussion】

1. What are the basic traits of American literature?

2. Describe the main figures of contemporary American literature.

3. Describe the main achievements of American literature.

# Unit 18

# Cinema

The story of American movies traces its beginnings to the 19th century, but the industry really was a child of the 20th century. In the United States, inventor extraordinaire Thomas A. Edison's preoccupation with capturing moving objects on film fueled a $44 billion industry in 2006. From the five second black-and-white film *Fred Ott's Sneeze*, which featured Edison's assistant in 1894, the movie industry burst on the entertainment scene.

While the newspaper industry fought off competition from other media, the film industry's story is one of adaptation. Television, VCRs, DVDs, and other innovations could have decimated the film industry, but instead, it has thrived. The movie industry is a vital and vibrant industry that in the United States generates about 600 films each year. It is the United States' biggest export.

Filmmaking in the United States began modestly enough. Edison's Black Maria studio in West Orange, New Jersey, began producing film shorts, including a 20-second popular item, *The Kiss*. It created a furor and was notable for starting the discussion of censorship in regard to film as early as 1896. Early short films found an audience in cities at Kinetescope Parlors, which allowed viewers to see snippets of film by paying 25 cents, an exorbitant price at the time.

*The Great Train Robbery* was produced in 1903 by one of Edison's employees, Edwin S. Porter. He was notable for its creation of the modern film technique of using several camera positions for the same scene and then editing the film to enhance suspense, create tension, and improve the narrative. That 12 minute silent film also gave rise to the western film genre.

Films found a home at the nickelodeon, movie houses where viewers could see a series of short films beginning about 1905. They spread quickly around the United States, creating a huge demand for new films. Thus an industry was born. By 1909, there were 9,000 movie theaters in the United States. America was not alone in its interest in the budding film industry. Foreign films like *The Cabinet of Dr. Caligari* in 1919 (from Germany) and others found audiences in the United States and contributed to the developing artistic techniques that included both direction and camera work.

The silent film era included the development of serial stories that were updated periodically, a precursor to the soap operas of radio and television. Notable in this group was *The Perils of Pauline*, which began in 1914 and featured a damsel in distress who was regularly saved from burning buildings, railroad tracks, and the side of a cliff. The series played on the concept of a cliffhanger ending that brought the viewers back to see the next episode.

The impact of sound in film history is enormous. Audiences flocked to *The Jazz Singer* and clamored for more. Actors whose voices did not lend them to film were swept aside in favor of those who were photogenic and whose voices were pleasant.

Movie-making grew into an industry that was centered around a few powerful studios. The studio system, as it came to be known, revolved around five companies: RKO, Paramount, 20th Century Fox, MGM, and Warner Brothers. Most of the financially successful films of the 1930s and 1940s were produced and distributed through these studios.

Despite the desperate financial situation of many Americans during the Great Depression of the 1930s, people went to the movies. Whether it was to escape their dreary existence, or live vicariously through the exotic lives of film stars, or merely to pass the time for a few hours, Americans loved the movies. As movie production and techniques became more sophisticated, the film industry became the leviathan of the entertainment industry—about 80 million people (more than half the U.S. population) went to the movies every week. Films like *Gone with the Wind* and *The Wizard of Oz* in 1939 showcased the industry's storytelling and techniques in living color.

The 1930s also saw the introduction of feature-length animation, most notably the work of master animator Walt Disney. Disney Studio's foray into filmmaking began with *Snow White and the Seven Dwarfs* in 1937 and continued with such instant classics as *Pinocchio* (1940) and *Sleeping Beauty* (1959), to name a few. Even after Disney's death in 1966, and into the new millennium, Disney Studios continued its preeminent position among animators with films like *The Lion King* (1994), *Beauty and the Beast* (1991), and *Tarzan* (1999).

World War II saw the film industry become an arm of U.S. propaganda. Some leading directors, including Frank Capra and John Ford, actually made films for the government. Stars like Clark Gable, who actually joined the army, and his wife, Carol Lombard, who died in a plane crash during a campaign to sell war bonds, typified Hollywood patriotism during the war.

As the influence of Hollywood spread around the world, filmmaking branched into many genres. Musicals were made possible when sound was introduced in 1927; films like *Singing in the Rain* in 1952 and *The Sound of Music* in 1965 are still considered classics. Musicals are still a viable genre. *Chicago* won the Academy Award in 2002, while *Dreamgirls* was critically acclaimed in 2006.

The romantic comedy genre made stars of Cary Grant, Doris Day, Rock Hudson, and Jimmy Stewart beginning in the 1930s. Moviegoers came to expect nailbiting suspense films whenever Alfred Hitchcock directed. His films, including *Rear Window*, *The Thirtynine Steps*, *Vertigo*, and *North by Northwest*, delivered spinetingling fear in viewers. Director John Ford and star John Wayne typified the western genre, while Frank Capra focused on uplifting, happy endings typified by the still popular Christmas classic *It's a Wonderful Life* or the patriotic and inspirational *Mr. Smith Goes to Washington*.

It would be remiss not to note the contributions of current day directors and actors. Director George Lucas's six part *Star Wars* epic revived the science fiction genre with the release of the first film, *Star Wars*, in 1977. Steven Spielberg is one of the foremost contemporary directors and producers, whose oeuvre includes 1975's *Jaws*; 1981's *Raiders of the Lost Ark*, which launched Harrison Ford to superstardom; and 1993's best picture, *Schindler's List*, which also won him his first Academy Award for Best Director.

Other leading directors of contemporary Hollywood included Woody Allen, Martin Scorsese, Oliver Stone, Spike Lee, Penny Marshall, and Quentin Tarantino. Among movie actors in 2007, Keanu Reeves raked in about $206 million for his work in the *Matrix* sequels; Tom Cruise, Tom Hanks, and Jack Nicholson were also good dealmakers by insisting on a percent of the box office. While other media compete for Americans' time and can lure them away from theaters, the movies are still king. In 2006, the Motion Picture Association reported that the total U.S. box office take came to $9.49 billion, with *Pirates of the Caribbean: Dead Man's Chest* pulling in $423 million. Yet while going to the movies is still a viable activity, Americans are increasingly staying home to watch their flicks. In the United States, 37 percent preferred to watch movies in the comfort of their own home, according to the Motion Picture Association. That trend began in the 1980s, when the VCR first was made available in the United States. Video stores allowed consumers to rent relatively newly released movies to watch at home. The technology shifted in the late 1990s to DVDs, but the home market remained strong. Cable television also entered the fray with pay perview technology that allowed consumers to watch feature films and on demand offerings.

The story of film censorship in the United States is almost as old as the industry itself. As early as 1907, nickelodeons were shut down for allowing children to view inappropriate short films. The film industry wasted no time policing itself. By 1916, the National Association of the Motion Picture Industry was formed to oversee film content, and when that failed, filmmakers created the Motion Picture Producers and Distributors of America, led by former postmaster William H. Hays. The association accepted a Production Code, which came to be known as the Hays Code, in 1930. This self-censorship initiative was responsible for shaping the treatment of sex and violence in Hollywood in the 1930s. Some did not think it went far enough.

The Catholic Legion of Decency was formed in 1934 to combat what it believed was a corruption of morals by the film industry. The list created by the Legion condemned certain movies it deemed inappropriate for anyone. Others it listed as appropriate for children or for adults. The list lasted until 1978 and condemned such movies as *From Russia with Love*, *Rosemary's Baby*, and *Grease*.

In 1968, the Motion Picture Association of America created its own voluntary film rating system, which is still in use today. The initial system included the ratings G for general audiences, M for mature audiences, R for restricted (under 16 not admitted without a parent or guardian), and X for no one under 17 admitted. The system has been finetuned over the years to include the PG (parental guidance suggested) and PG13 (parental guidance suggested for age 13).

While the earliest film actors were anonymous, the star system emerged during the 1920s. The Marx Brothers epitomized comedy; Jean Harlow was a vamp; Edward G. Robinson was a gangster; Bela Legosi was typecast in horror films; Cary Grant and Clark Gable were two of the earliest leading men. As Hollywood actors and actresses became celebrities, they were able to command large sums of money for their work. Hollywood became known as Tinseltown.

The success of the 1939 film *Gone with the Wind* ushered in a golden age for Hollywood. The movie, based on the runaway best seller by Margaret Mitchell, won 10 Academy Awards in 1939 and held the record for making money for many years, before contemporary ticket prices knocked it out. It still holds the record for the most tickets sold.

The Academy Awards to recognize achievement in film were begun in 1929 in Los Angeles. The winners were given a distinctive gold statuette of a man to honor their achievements. Legend has it that film star Bette Davis, who won two and was nominated 10 times, dubbed the statue "Oscar" because it reminded her of her first husband. Held annually in the spring, the Oscars attract an international audience and generate hoopla for celebrities, who prance along a red carpet into the auditorium.

While other countries have established notable film industries, most especially Japan, India, and Italy, American films are the undisputed world leader. In fact, as movie going habits shifted with television viewing and then the VCR technology that brought the theaters into homes, American filmmakers turned increasingly to the export market to make up the financial difference. By 2007, more than half of American film revenues came from the foreign market, forcing filmmakers to pay attention to how a movie will play with foreign audiences. It was by no means a oneway street. Increasingly, Americans were open to viewing foreign films. The Chinese film *Crouching Tiger, Hidden Dragon* grossed $128 million in the United States in 2000.

## ▶ A Short Story ◀

### Star Wars

*Star Wars* is an American epic space opera franchise, centered on a film series created by George Lucas. It depicts the adventures of various characters "a long time ago in a galaxy far, far away."

The franchise began in 1977 with the release of the film *Star Wars* (later subtitled *Episode IV: A New Hope* in 1981), which became a worldwide pop culture phenomenon. It was followed by the successful sequels *The Empire Strikes Back* (1980) and *Return of the Jedi* (1983); these three films constitute the original Star Wars trilogy. A prequel trilogy was released between 1999 and 2005, which received mixed reactions from both critics and fans. A sequel trilogy began in 2015 with the release of *Star Wars: The Force Awakens*. All seven films were nominated for Academy Awards (with wins going to the first two films) and have been commercial successes, with a combined box office revenue of over U.S. $7.5 billion, making *Star Wars* the third highest-grossing film series. Spin-off films include the animated *Star Wars: The Clone Wars* (2008) and *Rogue One* (2016), the latter of which is the first in a planned series of anthology films.

The series has spawned an extensive media franchise including books, television series, computer and video games, theme park attractions, and comic books, resulting in significant development of the series' fictional universe. *Star Wars* also holds a Guinness World Records title for the "Most successful film merchandising franchise". In 2015, the total value of the *Star Wars* franchise was estimated at US$ 42 billion, making *Star Wars* the second highest-grossing media franchise of all time.

In 2012, The Walt Disney Company bought Lucasfilm for US $ 4.06 billion and earned the distribution rights to all subsequent *Star Wars* films, beginning with the release of *The Force Awakens* in 2015. The former distributor, 20th Century Fox, retains the physical distribution rights for the first two *Star Wars* trilogies, owns permanent rights for the original 1977 film and continues to hold the rights for the prequel trilogy and the first two sequels to *A New Hope* until May 2020. Walt Disney Studios owns digital distribution rights to all the *Star Wars* films, excluding *A New Hope* .

## ··· *Exercises* ···

【Fill in the Blanks】

1. The early American films were used mainly to showcase America's _____, news items, and social events.

2. The first of these early American movie theaters, which opened in Pittsburgh in 1905, was called "_____."

3. Hollywood had entered into an artistic _____ by the late 1930s, producing annually over four hundred feature films.

4. Black people also had taken part in American popular culture prior to _____.

5. Among the 1930s' attractions was the 1939 film _____, a spectacular epic starring _____ and Vivian Leigh.

【Multiple Choices】

1. Films made in the 1920s have the following characteristics except _____.

    A. cynicism               B. sensuality

    C. democratic optimism    D. rampant materialism

2. Which studio was not part of the five "majors"?

    A. Fox.      B. MGM.      C. Warner Brothers.      D. Universal.

3. New genre films emerged since the 1950s. Which one especially catered to the needs of the youngsters?

    A. Horror films.              B. Science fiction films.

    C. Rock 'n' roll films.       D. Westerns.

4. Which became the new standard for consumer video since the late 1990s?

    A. DVDs.                 B. VHS tapes.

    C. CDs.                  D. LPs.

5. Which of the following genre films does *Jaws* belong?

    A. A suspense picture.       B. A science fiction film.

    C. A horror film.            D. A western film.

【Discussion】

1. Briefly introduce the history of American movie.

2. What are the main functions of Hollywood in the process of the development of American movie?

3. Describe the style of American movie-makers.

# Theater

Early American theater mimicked European performances and acting techniques. Although records are incomplete for this period, most theater scholars name Anthony Aston as the first professional actor in America in 1703. (Aston was, however, preceded by Native American spiritualists who regularly played roles in rituals.) Williamsburg, Virginia, boasted a dance school and theater as early as 1716. Philadelphia constructed a playhouse where Pickleherring pieces, a genre of acting that followed European clowning techniques, were performed. The City of Brotherly Love was the center of colonial theater activity until 1825. Walter Murray and Thomas Kean took simple shows on tour through many of the colonies. Charleston surged ahead of the other colonial cities with a new theater constructed in 1736; at that time, the New York City theater scene paled in comparison.

The London Company of Comedians (later changed to the American Company), led by Lewis Hallan Sr., and then by David Douglas, held a monopoly on professional theater productions from 1752 until 1755, when Hallan's son took over his father's part of the team. The pair constructed and revitalized theaters throughout the colonies, who held that plays advocated immoral behavior (despite the subtitle A Moral Dialogue attached to most plays' titles). Douglas built two of the most important theaters in the colonies in New York in the 1760s and put on the first play written by a native playwright. The Continental Congress banned all stage performances in October 1774, but American playwrights continued working even as British troops captured cities and put on their own military performances in the colonial theaters. The period after the Revolutionary War was a time of rapid theater construction, as acting companies returned and new troupes were formed. French-speaking theaters were constructed in New Orleans and Charleston. New York challenged Philadelphia for the title of theater capital of the colonies but was not recognized as a serious contender until 1800.

As the United States acquired land with each act passed by Congress beginning in 1815, theaters and acting companies moved into the new territories. Floating theaters were located on showboats that traveled the Mississippi River. The Boston Museum began its stock touring company in 1841, and the troupe prospered for nearly 50 years. San Francisco received professional acting troupes from the east in 1850; actors were well compensated for their long journey and for facing dangers in the western territories.

The 1850s established a clear American tradition on the stage, with the high period for theater profits running from the Civil War era until 1915. Matilda Heron, an actress with an overtly dramatic technique, rose to fame in 1857 in historical costume dramas that were all the rage. Most of the plays, would be considered campy with their stilted, unnatural dialogue, but theater moved toward a more realistic approach in the following decades. The melodrama, a style that rose to popularity in the 1860s, always had a dramatic turning point such as the rescue of someone (usually a damsel tied to railroad tracks). One of the most famous of the moral plays was *Uncle Tom's Cabin*, which opened in 1852 with a mostly white cast in blackface. Blacks played other roles, but not the major parts in the production. Translations of French plays were also popular during this decade.

By the 1870s, plays about social issues were in vogue; comedies and dramas covered timely issues. Territorial expansion and the rise of the American West was a popular topic that aligned with the phenomenal sales of the dime novels, purportedly chronicling the lives and times of gunslingers, outlaws, and mysterious natives of the new territories. A star system developed beginning in the 1880s, with Edwin Booth, Edwin Forrest, and Charlotte Cushman commanding top salaries. John Drew and Georgina Drew Barrymore (an ancestor of the contemporary Drew Barrymore) followed.

Popular actors, prior to the turn of the century, regularly built their own theaters to showcase their talents.

Theater fans make a clear distinction between regional theater and the rural theater of summer stock, even though summer stock usually attracted audiences from a specific region. The distinction between the two is that regional theater was considered highbrow and summer stock lowbrow. Regional theater had professional actors, playhouses, and productions, while summer stock frequently used amateur actors, some of whom even paid to be involved in the performances. This should not diminish the significance of summer stock in building culture in rural America. As the once-massive Chautauqua circuit faded, summer stock theater rose to popularity in the 1920s and 1930s in the Northeast. Professional and amateur actors, stage crews, production designers, and directors were hired each summer to put on a group of plays, or a new play each week, in independent theaters that attracted upper-and middle-class vacationers from nearby summer resorts. Some theater historians claim that summer stock is the only true regional theater in the United States. English and early American theaters had resident actor stocks, but summer stock did not operate year-round. English theater companies did not have a separate group to be involved exclusively in summer productions.

Summer stock theaters operated during the months of June to September, from Maine to Virginia to Pennsylvania in the west. By the 1930s, some houses offered touring companies, and most had a permanent playhouse. Summer stock venues ranged from converted barns to small theaters constructed specifically for the permanent summer company. Early playhouses used local talent, then shifted to the star system that employed a featured actor (often on hiatus from Broadway shows that were closed during the hot summer months of July and August), and finally used a combination of the two during the 1960s. Playwright Eugene O'Neill premiered his first work in summer stock at the Provincetown Wharf Theatre in Cape Cod, Massachusetts, in 1918. Summer stock's popularity first came with the automobile, which allowed escape from the summer heat of the city, and the new road system that made getting to rural resorts easy.

American theater came into its own during World War I. European plays and actors were not visiting as frequently, and the influence from Europe on American staging and plays was minimal. The First International Exhibition of Modern Art, held in 1913 at the building that normally housed the 67th Regiment Armory in New York City, with its American and European paintings and sculpture, challenged the traditional definition of art and encouraged people working on the stage, and in set and costume design, to take greater artistic risks. The Broadway theaters in New York became the center of America's theater world at the turn of the century, routinely taking productions from Philadelphia and Chicago.

During the Depression years of the 1930s, theaters received funds from the Federal Theatre Project, a part of President Franklin Delano Roosevelt's Works Progress Administration (WPA) that provided salaries for unemployed designers, writers, actors, and stage workers. The program, under the direction of Hallie Flanagan, came under fire in the late 1930s for employing members of the Socialist and Communist parties and for producing works that attacked big business. *The Living Newspaper*, a short-lived experiment in theater design, was abandoned when federal funding was abruptly cut after elected officials objected to criticism from the quickly written plays that interpreted the economic, political, and social issues from the front pages of the news. The electric industry was mocked for the high prices for service in the play *Power*.

The period from 1900 to 1932 saw theaters in New York City dwindle from 5,000 houses to only 132. Travel was limited during the Depression and World War II due to fuel shortages and restrictions on hard-to-find products such as natural rubber. After World War II, there was a resurgence in theater and summer stock productions. The decades between 1945 and 1965 are considered the brightest of the Broadway stage. The plays or musicals of Lerner and Loewe, Tennessee Williams, Rogers and Hammerstein, William Inge, and Arthur Miller were performed to small audiences in theaters that were built decades before, without expensive audio and lighting equipment:

the play was the thing. Musicals starring Shirley MacLaine, dramas with headliners such as Geraldine Page and Marlon Brando, and plays and shows that remain on Broadway in revivals today—*West Side Story, Cat on a Hot Tin Roof,* and *A Streetcar Named Desire* —were first performed in this period.

During their heyday, the summer theaters brought recent Broadway hits, comedies, and melodramas to new audiences. Between 1930 and 1960, summer stock employed more theater folk than any other venue in America, including Broadway. The Ford Foundation, under the direction of W. Mac-Neil Lowry, gave generously to the arts, but by the 1960s, the middle classes could travel by air to exotic locations, and attendance at summer stock venues and on Broadway fell. Many small Broadway theaters and summer stock venues could not attract enough revenue and were abandoned. A few regional theaters continue to perform historic dramas; Roanoke Island, North Carolina, Tamiment in the Pocono Mountains, and Green Mansions in the Adirondack Mountains remain in operation today.

Funding has always been a concern for theater productions, and the federal government created assistance in the form of the National Endowment for the Arts. It provided nearly $3 million in grants in 1966 and increased the figure each year until it reached over $162 million in 1995. After a long period of increases, the legislature was motivated by constituent letters over funding for art that offended some sensibilities and took a red pen to the arts budget, reducing funding to $99 million. During the period from 2004 through 2007, the funding remained around $124 million for future years.

American theater frequently experimented with avant-garde productions in the decades between 1920 and 1970, notably in theaters appealing to workers and union members. The Workers' Theater, Workers Drama League (later called the New Playwrights Theater), and the Theater Union put on performances to illustrate the struggles of the working class and promote a political transformation in America. The 1950s and the early 1960s saw little experimentation in the mainstream theater, but the late 1960s into the 1970s were much different. The Open Theater performances attempted to eliminate the invisible barrier between the actors and the audience and meld them together in plays such as *The Mutation Show* by Joseph Chaikin (produced off Broadway) and the Bread and Puppet Theater's *Fire*, which challenged America's position as aggressor in Vietnam. Sitting was not an option at *Fire*, as symbolic masked figures were allowed the freedom to move through the audience in a theater devoid of traditional seats.

There were only 23 regional theaters in the United States in the early 1960s, but by 2007, the number had mushroomed to over 1,800. Many are new structures with state-of-the-art lighting and sound systems. The smaller venues offer new playwrights an opportunity to get produced without the large financial losses a Broadway production could incur. Some famous writers prefer to test a new play in a small venue before opening a Broadway play or touring production. The top five regional theaters year in and year out in the United States include the Old Globe Theatres in San Diego, California; the South Coast Repertory in Orange County, California; the Goodman Theater in Chicago; the American Repertory Theater in Cambridge, Massachusetts; and the Guthrie Theater of Minneapolis, Minnesota.

The Guthrie continues to lead all small theaters in the country, with 32,000 season ticket subscribers. Playwrights such as Arthur Miller have premiered works on this stage with the company's seasoned actors. Theater founder Sir Tyrone Guthrie directed the first production, Shakespeare's tragedy *Hamlet*. The project grew out of a plan that Guthrie made with Oliver Rea and Peter Zeisler to establish a resident acting company and a venue to stage the classics, far away from Broadway's glare and pressure for success. The group did not select Minneapolis; in fact, the city selected the Guthrie planners. A Drama Section appeal in the *New York Times* brought offers from seven cities, but Minneapolis brought more than interest: it brought funding and cooperation with the theater arts program at the University of Minnesota. The T. B. Walker Foundation donated land and a sizable fund to be put toward the theater's construction. With Ford and McKnight Foundation grants providing monies for construction and operation, the Guthrie opened in 1963. The focus of the Guthrie has changed with the appointment of each new artistic director, but over the decades, the theater has been given a Tony Award for outstanding contributions to American theater and is routinely included in lists of America's best regional theaters. It now includes a touring theater group and a lab theater that explores the works of contemporary playwrights.

While regional and local theaters have gained audiences, Broadway fans have seen a decline in offerings since the mid-1960s. Stage productions have been transformed into films on a regular basis since the beginnings of the film industry, but playwrights have also taken films and transformed them into stage shows. The most notable series of successful plays adapted for screen are those of the Marx Brothers. Brothers Harpo, Chico, Groucho, Gummo, and Zeppo clowned their way to Broadway success in nearly a dozen shows. However, only two of the recreated stage plays, *Duck Soup* (1933) and *A Night at the Opera* (1935)—productions not usually noted as high art—are listed by the American Film Institute among the 100 most significant films in movie history.

*The Wiz*, a restaging of the 1939 classic movie *The Wizard of Oz*, won Tony Awards for choreography and costume design in 1975. The stage version of the 1951 film *Sunset Boulevard* received critical acclaim when it was introduced in London and then toured the United States in the 1980s. More recently, modern films that are box office successes without critical acclaim have made their way to Broadway. Legally Blonde and Hairspray join remakes of Disney animated features and have drawn a new generation of theatergoers. Popular music from the 1960s is currently featured on Broadway in *Jersey Boys* (chronicling the life of the Four Seasons singing group) and *Dream Girls* (a fictionalized portrayal of Motown's Supremes). *High School Musical*, a popular Disney television movie with a plotline revolving around musical theater, has drawn teen and "tween" wannabes to Broadway in droves. Broadway shows are experiencing longer lives for productions and musicals. *Cats*, *Chicago*, *Beauty and the Beast*, and *Phantom of the Opera* are currently in contention for record-breaking runs on Broadway.

## ▶ A Short Story ◀

### Matilda Agnes Heron

Matilda Agnes Heron (1830－1877) was a popular mid-19th century actress in the United States, best known for her role in the play *Camille.*

Born in Ireland in 1830, Heron emigrated to the United States in 1842, and lived in Philadelphia. Starting in 1851 she began appearing professionally in plays. In 1853 she traveled to California and gained popularity. In 1854, she was married to lawyer Henry Herbert Byrne in San Francisco, but the union lasted but a few months.

While in Paris in 1855, Heron saw the popular play *La Dame aux camélias* (*The Lady of the Camellias*), and decided to present her own version, in English, in America. The resulting *Camille*, for which she is best known, had its New York debut in January 1857 at Wallack's Theatre. Edward Askew Sothern played the role of the lover. Of her role in *Camille*, prominent theater critic William Winter later wrote: "Other parts she acted; that one she lived." She was known for her emotional style of acting.

In 1857, Heron wed composer Robert Stoepel (they separated in 1869). During the 1861–1862 season Heron wrote *The Belle of the Season* and starred in it at the Winter Garden. In 1863, she gave birth to a daughter, Helen Wallace Stoepel, better known as Bijou Heron, who became an actress herself. By the late 1860s, and as her health began to wane, Matilda Heron receded from the spotlight and taught acting. A big benefit show was done to raise funds for her in January 1872, which included Edwin Booth, Jules Levy, John Brougham, and Laura Keene.

She died in New York City on March 7th, 1877. Her reported last words were "Tilly never did harm to anyone—poor Tilly is so happy."

## ▪▪▪ Exercises ▪▪▪

【Fill in the Blanks】

1. Theater fans make a clear distinction between ＿＿＿＿ theater and the

_____ theater of summer stock.

2. The President _____ Works Progress Administration (WPA) that provided salaries for unemployed designers, writers, actors and stage workers.

3. American theater frequently experimented with _____ productions in the decades between 1920 and 1970.

4. A Drama Section appeal in the _____ brought offers from seven cities.

5. The Theater Union put on performances to illustrate the struggles of the working class and promote a _____ transformation in America.

【Multiple Choices】

1. Charleston surged ahead of other colonial cities with a new theater constructed in _____.
   A. 1735          B. 1736          C. 1737          D. 1738

2. In what format was *Avatar* released worldwide in 2009?
   A. 2D format.     B. IMAX format.   C. 3D format.     D. IMAX 3D format.

3. Which of the following generation did rock music cater to?
   A. The baby-boomer generation.      B. The Lost Generation.
   C. Generation X.                    D. The Beat Generation.

4. The period from 1900 to 1932 saw theaters in _____ City dwindle from 5,000 houses to only 132.
   A. New York       B. Chicago        C. Houston        D. Detroit

5. Three powerful female performers emerged to great popular success in the 1990s, except _____.
   A. Tracy Chapman                    B. Sinead O' Connor
   C. Sarah Mclachlan                  D. Taylor Swift

【Discussion】

1. Why are American theaters still popular among the people?
2. Describe the developing history of American Theater.

## Unit 20

# Museum

The Founding Fathers of the United States did not envision the collection of art to be in the purview of government. For one thing, the United States began its existence completely broke and heavily in debt. For another, patronizing the arts surely must have smacked to them to be the stuff of popes, monarchs, and noblemen, all anathema in the new republic. Furthermore, they understood government to have a very small role in domestic life. In 1841, the National Institute was created in the Patent Office to oversee art and historical items the government had come to own. John Varden, its first curator, had begun collecting art privately, and his collection was added to what the government already had. The institute was disbanded in 1862 and its collections sent to the Smithsonian Institution, which was founded in 1846. After a fire at the Smithsonian Castle in 1865, most of the art was loaned out to other museums well into the twentieth century. A 1906 court case caused the Smithsonian's art collection to be named a National Gallery of Art, a heightened status that encouraged donations of new artworks.

The federal government's entrance into art collecting and museums had been, for the most part, accidental to this point, and certainly unenthusiastic. There was no proper federal art museum until financier Andrew W. Mellon donated his European art collection to the United States in 1937, and his foundation paid for the building, designed by Eliel Saarinen, to house it. In 1941, the National Gallery of Art opened on the mall in the nation's capital. The Mellon family and foundation also donated funds for the gallery's East Building, designed by I. M. Pei. It opened in 1978. Varden's original collection, greatly enlarged, is housed in the newly renovated Old Patent Office Building and is known as the Smithsonian American Art Museum. The collection includes the works of more than 7,000 American artists.

The National Gallery of Art was not the first federal art museum. The Smithsonian's first fine art museum was the Freer Gallery. Charles Lang Freer (1854-1919) made a fortune as a railroad car manufacturer in Detroit. He was an avid collector of Asian art and Buddhist sculpture. He gave his collection to the nation along with the money to build a museum. The Freer Gallery opened in 1923. The Arthur M. Sackler Gallery of Asian Art is connected to the Freer and was opened in 1987 to house Dr. Sackler's (1913-1987) gift to the country.

The movement to establish art museums went all over the country. The Los Angeles County Museum of Art, now with extensive and diverse collections, was established in 1910 without a collection. The Museum of Fine Arts in Houston, Texas, opened in 1924, the result of 24 years of work by the Houston Public School Art League. Today, America has more than 1,700 art museums, and some of its most significant ones were founded in the twentieth century. Wealthy art collectors and patrons Mary Sullivan, Abby Aldrich Rockefeller, and Lillie P. Bliss founded the Museum of Modern Art in 1929 in New York City because the large museums were reluctant to collect modern and contemporary art. Thus was established one of the world's premier art museums. Major Duncan Phillips and his wife, Marjorie, left their Washington, D.C. home in 1930 for another residence, turning their old home into an art museum. The Phillips Collection is a major institution of modern art and its origins. Gertrude Vanderbilt Whitney founded the Whitney Museum in 1931, with her own collection of twentieth-century American art as its foundation. The Frick Collection was created and endowed by Henry Clay Frick, the Pittsburgh steel magnate. When he died in 1919, he requested that his New York City residence become a museum to house his hundreds of artworks, including old masters, after the death of his wife. The museum opened to the public in 1935.

Oilman J. Paul Getty opened the J. Paul Getty Museum at his Malibu,

California, ranch in 1954. Since 1984, the trustees of his estate have sought to promote Getty's belief in art as a humanizing influence by expanding the museum's programs beyond the original campus with the Getty Center in Los Angeles. The collections have been greatly enhanced beyond Getty's collection of antiquities and European paintings and furniture. In 1937, industrialist Solomon R. Guggenheim established his eponymous foundation to operate museums based on his collections of nonobjective art. While Solomon's artworks were put into traveling shows and his niece Peggy Guggenheim was making her own name in the art world as a dealer and patron, the first permanent home for the Guggenheim opened in Frank Lloyd Wright's famous New York City landmark in 1959. The Kimbell Art Museum in Fort Worth, Texas, opened in a Louis I. Kahn-designed building in 1972. It was established through a foundation by entrepreneur Kay Kimbell, his wife, and his wife's sister and her husband. The museum houses a diverse collection reaching back to antiquity.

Traveling museum exhibits take important art throughout the country. The Museum of Contemporary Art (MoCA) in Cleveland, Ohio, recently exhibited some of the paintings of Dana Schutz (1976-) completed between 2002 and 2006. Schutz tried to extend reality into the imaginary in her paintings. These included selections from her series Self-Eaters. MoCA also exhibited two shows of Catherine Opie's (1961-) photographs, "1999" and "In and Around the House." The "1999" photographs were taken on a trip around the country in 1999; the photographs of the other show depict a close look at American life at home, with Opie's family as subjects. In an exhibit called Sarah Kabot: On the Flip Side, emerging Cleveland artist Sarah Kabot (1976-) had the opportunity to show her interest in the relationship between form and content through her art, which included transforming a spiral notebook into a new meaning.

In Houston, Texas, the Contemporary Arts Museum presented its patrons with the traveling exhibit Kiki Smith: A Gathering, 1980-2005. Smith's exploration of humanity and spirituality could be discovered in about 250 works in diverse media. In its Perspectives series, the museum gives artists their first opportunities for museum exhibition. Artists who have lately exhibited in this series include Michael Bise, who draws domestic scenes; Soody Sharifi, who photographs communities; Janaki Lennie, who paints cityscapes; and Demetrius Oliver, who is a Houston conceptual artist engaged in performance, sculpture, and photography. The Houston Museum also mounted a traveling retrospective of Sam Gilliam's (1933-) draped paintings. Gilliam took canvases off stretchers and walls, turning them into three-dimensional installations.

The Contemporary Art Center of Virginia in Virginia Beach featured Watering, an exhibition of 24 photographs by Elijah Gowin (1967-). Gowin used composite photos from the Internet that he built digitally into montages, and which he then, as negatives, put through a scanning and printing process to invoke contemporary meaning for the act of baptizing. The Butler Institute of American Art in Youngstown, Ohio, showed Lightboxes and Melts. Artist Ray Howlett (1940-) produced light sculptures using LED technology. The San Francisco Museum of Modern Art featured a nearly three-month run of the Drawing Restraint series, an ongoing work of art by Matthew Barney (1967-). It is a performance-based project that employs film, photography, drawing, sculpture, and video to investigate the idea that form comes out of struggle against resistance.

The attendance rate for art museums across the United States is 34.9 per-cent, which means that only about one in three Americans visits an art museum in a given year. There are regional variations, however, in attendance rates. New England (42.4%), the Mid-Atlantic (38.7%), and the Pacific Northwest with Hawaii (39.7%) exceed the national average. The attendance rate in the south Atlantic region is bolstered by Florida (35.5%), but its overall rate is only 30.5 percent. (This region includes the states of Florida, Georgia, South Carolina, North Carolina, Virginia, West Virginia, Maryland, and Delaware.) The west south central region outside of Texas, which exactly meets the national rate, has an attendance rate of only 26.5 percent. This region includes Texas as well as Oklahoma, Louisiana, and Arkansas. Art museum attendance in the mountain states (Montana, Idaho,

Wyoming, Utah, Nevada, Arizona, Colorado, and New Mexico) at 40 percent exceeds the national average. In the east south central region, including Kentucky, Tennessee, Mississippi, and Alabama, the attendance rate at art museums is a meager 24.8 percent. The Midwest generally meets the national rate. When participation rates in art experiences through television are considered, however, most regions come near or above the national rate of 45.1 percent. The east south central region is the notable exception at only 36.5 percent. The American Association of Museums reported in 2003 that median annual attendance for art museums totaled 61,312, whereas zoos had 520,935; science and technology museums had 183,417; arboretums and botanical gardens had 119,575; children's/youth museums had 85,088; and natural history museums had 64,768.

▶ *A Short Story* ▶

### Andrew William Mellon

Andrew William Mellon was an American banker, businessman, industrialist, philanthropist, art collector, and politician. From the wealthy Mellon family of Pennsylvania, he established a vast business empire before transitioning into politics. He served as United States Secretary of the Treasury from March 9th, 1921 to February 12th, 1932, presiding over the boom years of the 1920s and the Wall Street crash of 1929. A conservative Republican, Mellon lowered taxes and government spending in the aftermath of World War I.

The son of banker Thomas Mellon, Andrew Mellon quickly established himself in the financial world. He became an owner of the family banking business, T. Mellon&Sons, and branched out into other businesses. Mellon helped finance the establishment of Alcoa, the New York Shipbuilding Corporation, Old Overholt whiskey, and several other companies. By the 1920s, he was one of the richest people in the country, paying more in income taxes than all but two other American industrialists. Mellon also became a prominent philanthropist, helping to establish the National Gallery of Art and the Mellon Institute of Industrial Research, which now part of Carnegie Mellon University.

In 1921, Warren G Harding chose Mellon as his treasury secretary. Mellon would remain in office until 1932, serving under Harding, Calvin Coolidge, and Herbert Hoover, all three of whom were members of the Republican Party. Mellon sought to reduce federal taxation and debt. He favored cutting the federal estate tax as well as income taxes on top earners, though he also sought tax cuts for all income levels. His policies were enacted by Congress in the *Revenue Act of 1921*, the *Revenue Act of 1924*, and the *Revenue Act of 1926*. The national debt dropped dramatically during the 1920s, though it would rise again after 1929. Mellon also participated in international agreements such as the Mellon-Berenger Agreement, which reduced French debts from World War I.

Mellon became unpopular after the onset of the Great Depression. According to Hoover, Mellon advised him to avoid intervening in the ongoing economic crisis. In 1932, the United States House of Representatives began conducting impeachment hearings against Mellon. Before the conclusion of the proceedings, Mellon accepted appointment to the position of United States Ambassador to the United Kingdom. He served in that post for the remainder of Hoover's presidency before retiring from public office in 1933.

## ▪▪▪ Exercises ▪▪▪

【Fill in the Blanks】

1. Tin Pan Alley was an area called _____ in New York City, which had been the major center for _____ .

2. The Mellon family and foundation also donated funds for the _____ Building.

3. The Smithsonian's first fine art museum was the _____ .

4. _____ took canvases off stretchers and walls, turning them into three-dimensional installations.

5. The American Association of Museums reported in _____ .

【Multiple Choices】

1. Charles Lang Freer made a fortune as a railroad car manufacturer in _____.

   A. Chicago        B. Detroit        C. New York        D. Boston

2. _____ is Walt Whitman's masterpiece.

   A. *The Waste Land*        B. *The Weary Blues*

   C. *Leaves of Grass*        D. *An American Tragedy*

3. Which invention marked the beginning of "The Age of Visual Information"?

   A. Newspapers.        B. The telegraph.

   C. Motion pictures.        D. Television.

4. Which of the following had the title "the Wizard of Menlo Park"?

   A. Bill Gates.        B. John Stevens.

   C. Thomas A. Edison.        D. Robert Fulton.

5. _____ produces light sculptures using LED technology.

   A. Sam Gilliam.        B. Ray Howlett.

   C. Elijah Gowin.        D. Kay Kimbell.

【Discussion】

1. What are the main contributions of American museums?
2. Describe the distinctive features of American museums.